He Speaks She Answers

By

Ellard Thomas

No part of this book may be reproduced, stored in a retrieval system, or transmitted by any means without the written permission of the author.

ISBN: 1-4033-4979-7 (e)
ISBN: 1-4033-4980-0 (sc)

Library of Congress Control Number: 2002093061

Printed in the United States of America
Bloomington, Indiana

This book is printed on acid-free paper.

1stBooks - rev. 12/21/04

To the poets and the art in which we know and love—poetry.

Thanks and Appreciation

I send my praises and thanks to God for choosing to bless me with the trials and triumphs that led to the development of this book. He is forever worthy of my praise.

I also thank my wife, Lakasha, an individual who helped me initially carry *He Speaks, She Answers* from merely its hobby phase to a published work. May God continue to send blessings upon you.

Last, but definitely not least, I give thanks to my mother, father, brothers and sisters, and all my other family and friends who have contributed to the efforts of assuring my success as an individual, and your contributions to a poet's dream. I thank you and I love you all.

Throughout time, fables, tales and stories have been based on hints or accents of truths. As meaningless and senseless as some of these may have been, these fictitious stories were often told to put a child to sleep or used to entertain youngsters gathered around campfires. For years, generations have told stories as accurately as possible to reflect the stories told by those preceding. However, there is one story that has been left untold—the story about Das Treymone—a man who finally finds love after living a deceitful and promiscuous lifestyle only to be forced to leave it. Join me as we together experience this man's quest in *He Speaks, She Answers*.

1
The Immutable Search

Dark is the sight, which conceals a man's hate, and the desires of his heart. Although many perceive him as warm and caring, his past is similar to an eerie autumn's night—chilly, black and mysterious. As a child, he saw and experienced many dreadful things—the beatings of his mother, the molestations of his sister, and the coerced separation of his family. Still controlled by the odious past he wishes to abandon, he's unable to trust or love any woman. Unfortunately, the brave and daring women who've shared their heart and body with him, found themselves alone and emotionally scarred. This was usually the outcome following a night of passion and temporary delight. Unfortunately, due to no fault of their own, these trusting women were not aware of the important knowledge they needed prior to their seeking this man's company. Beneath his success, charm and confidence lays a film of self-loath, anger and deceit. The paths on which he traveled towards adulthood were turned murky due to affliction's rains and misery's storms. The detours towards the promises of bliss led him to seduction's corners, where he was then dragged through the darkened tunnels of defile, dishonesty and distrust. Sadly and overlooked, this man's cry for help is hidden within the solemn howls of his smile. However, his love for lust is buried underneath the soot of his intelligent mind and his fragile heart. Mistakenly, these women who've given themselves to this man failed to know Das Treymone.

Young, ambitious, intelligent, and handsome, Das Treymone is a successful businessman who attracts women like mosquitoes to warm flesh. While some women are attracted to his magnetic personality and determination, others find themselves at the mercy of his majestic appearance and seductive, white smile. His subtle eyes mesmerize all who look into them. Some individuals believe men should envy such a man. However, although blessed with riches by his hard work and his investments, Das is also cursed. His ability to love is a gift which was taken away from him after being hurt by the women he cared for most. Thus leading to his insatiable appetite for unemotional intimacy. Capable of satisfying his sexual urges by sleeping with various women of his choice, Das decides the morning following a passionate night with his 58th victim he no longer has the desire to use women for his own sexual pleasures. Hence, he sells his printing business and escapes his indecent ways by moving to Dalay with his brother Kristoffe. After purchasing a four-bedroom house, overlooking the ocean, he tries to find peace within himself.

For six months, Das enjoys his seclusion from civilization as he deals with his emotional issues. Each day he sits on his bedroom balcony and writes in his journal. Each night, following conversation with his brother, he cries as he reflects on his past. Although content with being alone, he still has an unfulfilled desire to be a good man for a special woman. Realizing he has rid himself a great many of his emotional pains, he decides the time to find a special woman has come.

During an 1884, Dalay spring evening, Das and Kristoffe speak of memories past as they sit at the kitchen table. In the midst of their laughs and jokes, Das detours from the conversation at hand and asks his brother a series of questions.

"Kristoffe, can a man attain knowledge from a woman when he is considered the head of his household, the king of his castle and ordained as a leader? As a woman has been taught, can he, too, be submissive without losing his strength in his woman's eyes?"

Kristoffe stares at Das for a moment then shakes his head.

"Das, you have become this peculiar person whom lately I don't know. Each day you speak as if you're losing your complicated sense of touch. At least you can do, since you've dragged me here to the middle of almost nowhere, is act like my old brother—the brother that didn't speak like this. My single answer to all of your questions is no! Women are weak, and there are only a few reasons for their existence!"

"Really, Kristoffe? Entertain me!"

"Das, women are here in this world to make sure our food is well prepared, to bear our children, and to please us in every way, and, in any fashion we so desire. Therefore, to learn from a woman is incredulous and ridiculous!"

Das stares at his brother for a moment. An awkward smile appears on his face.

"Kristoffe, after your amusing, yet dysfunctional anecdotes, I'm happy that I brought you to Dalay. The general population should thank me for removing someone like you from its circulation. Truthfully, I despise those who answer no to my questions. I am a man filled with rage, hurt, and deceit; however, I am empty and would simply like a woman who I can provide for emotionally without having to be indecent."

Kristoffe looks inquisitively at his brother.

"Das. Maybe it's your past that has come to haunt you, or it's this change to finally be humble that has come to taunt you. Each day I wander who you are."

Following a head nod, Das excuses himself from the table then runs full speed up the stairs, darting into his room. After a lonely sigh, he opens his balcony window then grabs a pen and stationery from his desk. Once seated, he closes his eyes and utters a prayer.

"Father, who watches me from the Heavens, oh how I wish you would grant me an equal similar to the dame you provided Adam—

Send to me a Madame who will be untouched like that of Mary, and, who may prepare me for all of life's hidden enchantments!

For what reason have I been planted on this earth filled with hurt, anxiety and years of resentment?

Bring to me a day where I shall long for nothing—may the suffering which I possess be soon abandoned!"

After his short prayer, Das brings his chair to the balcony and writes a letter. For a half an hour, he scribbles his feelings and all that he desires.

He Speaks

> "I sit on this balcony only to stare at the night's sun—
> beautiful, so filled with hope, romance and passion—
> I sit on this balcony, cold in despair, while watching the
> wrinkles in the watery sheet Mother Earth calls Ocean.
> I've long yearned for a more than normal woman with
> whom I can share my heart, my soul and my life—
> As loud as my heart may beat—furious and anxious—
> still it seems to be very, very quiet.
> I want to pursue a life that is humble and blissful;

however, what I've received is anxiety—
My eons of searching has led me to a reef, which is
an end to nothing— the start of my vanity.
Before I become the remains, which fertilize the earth,
I pray this letter reach her—
The woman whom I never had, a woman of whom I
dreamt, a woman pure of light and hope.

Yours truly, Das Treymone."

Upon finishing the letter, Das folds it then grabs a corked-bottle from underneath his bed. Carefully, he inserts the letter inside along with a return address then kisses the bottle. As if he doesn't have a moment to spare, he hurries down the stairs and tells Kristoffe he's going to the ocean. Kristoffe offers to accompany him, but Das rejects his company and begins his one-mile journey.

As Das nears the ocean made bluish-green from algae and the sunlight's angle, he clenches the glass envelope and utters a prayer.

"Father, who've protected me from life's altercations, I come to you as a crying child who hunger your grace and blessing. I beg that you allow this message to reach a woman to whom I may have meaning. As I toss this bottle into the ocean made by your tears, I ask that you guide it to a destination which keeps sacred a queen."

Das tosses the bottle into the glossy ripples. He watches quietly as the waves carry his protected message. Once the bottle disappears into the distance, he journeys home in joy. Immediately, upon his entrance into the house, Kristoffe approach him.

"Well, my brother, Das. Did you enjoy your journey?"

"If you must know, I did."

"I'm sure. Do you realize that you've been gone for nearly two hours?"

"I wasn't aware that I needed your permission to be away for a certain amount of time, Kristoffe. Perhaps the next time I saunter, I will take you along. How does that sound, my younger brother?"

Das laughs at Kristoffe's facial expression then tells him to fetch the playing cards. After Kristoffe returns, the two close the evening with wine drinking, conversation and card play.

Three weeks following the throwing of his letter into the ocean, Das continues his daily routine of writing and conversing with his brother. Unknowingly to him, his bottle washes onto a Santa Lucia shore. By mere coincidence, a young twenty-four-year-old woman on her daily walk along the ocean discovers it. Filled with curiosity, she picks up the bottle then reads the letter inside. Joy fills her as she completes each poetic sentence. Impressed by the soulfully written note, she feels the need to respond. And at the end of her stroll, she hurries home.

Upon entering her house, the young woman tells her mother about her finding. Her mother shakes her head at her daughter's discovery and, after a brief mother and daughter conversation, the young woman rushes to her room, pulling a notebook from her desk drawer. Afterwards, she lies on her bed and responds to Das.

She Answers

"My fair Das, today I've received your letter and
surprisingly my heart also yearns for another—
One who endures strength, sensitivity and passion, and
one who is not afraid of what the majority may think of
him. I, too, know loneliness as well as you do, but my
definition is when one gives her heart only to be hurt in
return—
Loneliness has become my friend after I've befouled
my bed with a man I believed was my equal, but he
shattered my hopes!
Loneliness is sitting in a dark room crying tears of
emptiness and then asking the sweet Lord for a light—
It is the position I've occupied my entire life—in all of
God's blessed days and each devil's night.
I sense by your words that you have been hurt more
than once, and they all by women—
Like a man, a woman can possess venom that can
slowly disable a man's heart forever.
I cannot say I have not hurt anyone—at least
anyone who didn't deserve it—
My virginity was taken at the loss of a struggle

5

by a man who I've called Uncle as a little girl.
I do know loneliness as you know it, and surely we can
defeat it; therefore, I pray that God lift his sword and
knight you—
Each day is a day to appreciate and learn from the one
prior, so I tell you to not let anything or anyone else
blind you.

Your new friend, Janicah Mi'Voir"

The morning after Janicah writes her letter, she runs down the
stairs, leaps onto her couch and stares through the window, waiting
impatiently for the mail handler. As the mail handler approaches her
house, Janicah rushes to the door and flings it open.

"Good morning, Monsieur Chati. How are you?"

"I am good, my fair Janicah. Why are you up so early? It's six
o'clock."

"I know I should be sleep, but I can't for I have a very important
letter that I must give you."

"For me?"

"No. Not this time. Maybe next time."

"Is this going to a man?"

"Aren't you nosey? And if it was?"

"I would read it."

"I trust you respect me enough to not read my letter, Monsieur
Chati."

Chati looks at the envelope then smiles at Janicah.

"Young lady, Janicah. I will make it my duty to have this sent
to Dalay as soon as I return to the station. It should arrive within a
week's time."

"Good. Now give me a hug and go away!"

After receiving her mother's mail, Janicah hugs Chati then
watches as he mounts his carriage. Within a matter of moments he
becomes an image in the morning. Upon shutting the door, Janicah
returns to her bedroom, mind occupied with thoughts of Das.

As Janicah continues to live her life in the same fashion prior to
receiving Das's letter, her letter arrives to Das's home in six days.
Early the sixth morning, Kristoffe awakes to thunder-like knocking.

Tired and bothered about having his sleep disturbed, he hobbles down the stairs and swings open the door.

"Justin," Kristoffe growls, "is it necessary to deliver the mail so early?"

"Kristoffe, for six months I've delivered the mail here at the same time. Must you ask me this question each time I come?"

"I wasn't aware that I've asked you this question prior to now."

"Yes, you have."

"Very well. What do you have for me?"

"Nothing. Today, I have a letter for your brother. It's from Santa Lucia."

"Santa Lucia? I'll take it."

Justin hands Kristoffe Das's letter then leaves. After Kristoffe closes the door, he hustles up the stairs then bursts into his deep-sleeping brother's room.

"Oh Das," Kristoffe tempts. "Wake up, dear brother. Some dame has written you. If you don't wake up, I will be tempted to read it."

Kristoffe sits on Das's bed then nudges his elbow into his brother's side.

"Get up, Das!"

Awakened by his brother's nudges, Das slowly sits up and snatches the envelope from Kristoffe's grasp.

"Kristoffe, leave me, please!"

"Why? Why can't you read the letter with me here?"

"Do I really need to answer that question?"

"I asked it, didn't I?"

"Allow me the peace for which I ask."

"Fine."

Kristoffe leaves the room. Das pulls the letter from the vanilla-scented envelope then reads it quietly to himself. Afterwards, he grabs his stationery then replies.

He Speaks

> "My sweet love, I've awakened to an envelope,
> which was brought to me by my brother—
> Its peculiar, vanilla scent is an essence
> I smelled like none other.

The night previous I prayed to our Father, which art
in Heaven hallowed be His name—
That before I enter His kingdom of righteousness, He
will throw forth a sign that I will love again.
My sweet Janicah, I hope this is one of the answers
to my prayers, and if so, I will now believe—
My place is possibly with you in bliss and not
underneath the ruins of pain and calamity.
For a heart that desires the same as my own, I'm willing
to negotiate obstacles and challenges—
I shall swim shark-infested waters, climb heaven-high
peak mountains, and walk barefoot through deserts.
My aim is to reshape this heart that has been crenellated
by this world's bitterness, selfishness and hate—
To make right what's been made wrong, and to feel the
warmth of a woman who is so intelligent and great."

After writing his letter to Janicah, Das calls Kristoffe in to his room. In a matter of seconds, Kristoffe appears in the doorway.

"What do you want?" Kristoffe snarls.

"I need you to do me a favor."

"What am I—a servant?"

"Only if that were true— any way, aside from joking, I need you to take this letter to the mail station."

"What? Why can't you have Justin do it tomorrow?"

"I prefer to have it done today."

"I don't see anything wrong with your arms and legs. Why don't you do it yourself?"

"Are you going to do this for me or not?"

Kristoffe stares at his brother, sighing as he edges toward him. With a smile on his face, Das hands Kristoffe the letter.

"By when would you like this mailed, Das?" Kristoffe grunts.

"No rush. However, right now is a good time."

"Hmm! I'll do it when I wake up."

"You're awake now."

"So true, yet, I'm going back to sleep."

"Fine. Leave the letter on the desk then come get it once you awake."

8

"Don't call my name again, okay?"

"Go back to sleep, Kristoffe."

After the pass of two hours, Kristoffe reenters Das's room.

"I'm up! Give me the damn letter."

"It's on the desk."

"Is there anything else I can do for you, majesty?"

"Just handle this simple task and your services will no longer be needed."

Kristoffe snatches the letter from the desk then leaves Das's room like a gust of wind. No longer tired, Das sits up, looks out his bedroom window, watching as his brother mount his horse. Once Kristoffe rides into the day, Das leaps out of bed and, with thoughts of Janicah on his mind, skips to the restroom where he readies a bath. While in the tub, he whispers.

> "Joy has finally come to my door when before it passed
> me like two strangers in the night—
> I can now see the light within the darkness of my past;
> however, one question of how long will it last still gives
> me fright.
> Twice I've searched for simplicity in agony's pile, and
> twice I've been left with discomfort and grief—
> Each day I've swayed to the dying tunes of hope and
> nearly found myself in the slums of my enemies.
> If this woman, I've written, is whom I've yearned in my
> dreams, I promise to live life to its fullest—
> And if she is my serenity from my God in heaven, I will
> be sure to be the man for others I couldn't."

Relaxed and energized from a warm bath, Das returns to his room and gets dressed. Afterwards, he waits downstairs for Kristoffe, mind consumed with thoughts of Janicah.

While Das continues to wait patiently for his brother, Kristoffe enters the house with a smile on his face. After closing the door, he advances towards his brother.

"Das, you won't believe who I saw at the mail station."

"Whom?"

"Do you remember the lady friend I had prior to moving here?"

"Donica?"

"No, the other one."

"I can't keep up. Tell me, whom?"

"Monique."

"Really? What is she doing in this area?"

"Believe it or not, she resides in Dalay."

"Just when I thought the world couldn't get smaller, it collapses on me."

Kristoffe joins his brother on the sofa and continues the conversation.

"Tonight—you and I—I and you are going out."

"Where and with whom?"

"Don't worry about where," Kristoffe grins, "but as with whom, we will be dining with Monique and her good friend, Jessica."

"I'm not sure if I want to go out, Kristoffe. I'll stay here."

"Sorry, but that is not an option, Das. Besides, you haven't been out since we moved here. I remember when you were always out until the break of dawn. Now you're different. All you want to do is write in your journal and, as of recently, think about this lady whom has written you."

"Her name is Janicah."

"I do not care to know your friend's name. I just want us to have fun like we did before your new self. By the way, doesn't someone owe me a favor?"

"That I do. By what time should I be ready?"

"The young dames will be here by nine…"

After conversation, Das and Kristoffe go about their day. Like usual, Das writes in his journal while Kristoffe works on his music and impatiently awaits 9:00 PM.

Nearing 8:30 PM, both handsomely dressed brothers exit his room, meeting the other at the bathroom door. Das smiles at his brother's gray suit choice; Kristoffe nods. Shortly after their quiet compliments, each brother enter the bathroom and finish prepping himself in the mirror.

"Now that's the Das I know," Kristoffe compliments, standing behind his brother while looking in the mirror. "Look at you. You're looking very sharp. That beige suit and those brown shoes—ladies will be all over you tonight!"

"My aim isn't to please anyone tonight, Kristoffe. I don't want the old me to take over."

"The old you? What do you mean—the old you?"

"Women have always been my weakness. For six months, I haven't so much talked to, or spent time with anyone other than you and the family."

"Now you're confusing me. Stop worrying about what you're going to do. I know exactly what I'm going to do. Tonight, after dinner and dancing, I will be bringing Monique here. Do I need to say what my intentions are?"

"Spare me the visual."

"I'm sure Jessica is going to want to come over tonight as well. If she does, what do you plan to do?"

"Nothing."

"Nothing?"

"Nothing. I don't know this woman!"

"All the better for you to do whatever it is you want."

"Interesting, young brother. Very interesting."

Following their final grooming session and conversation regarding the evening, Das and Kristoffe stride arrogantly down the stairs. Both take a seat on the sofa, conversing as they await the women's arrival.

At nine o'clock, soft thumps come from the front door. Kristoffe leaps up then advances to the door. Before opening it, he looks at Das.

"How do I look?"

"The same as you did upstairs."

"I'll take that as your compliment."

When Kristoffe opens the door, his eyes widen at the sight before him. Monique's red dress over her voluptuous curves and caramel torso baffles him. Jessica's revealing black dress over her slender figure nearly causes him to faint. Realizing his brother is in need of assistance, Das approaches Kristoffe then places a hand on his shoulder.

"Kristoffe, aren't you going to introduce me to your friends?"

Kristoffe snaps out of his trance.

"Oh yes, where are my manners? Monique—Jessica, this is my brother, Das."

"Hello Das," Monique greets.

"Good evening, Das," Jessica follows.

"Good evening ladies," Das smiles. "You two are exceptionally beautiful. Your lovely appearance and your elegant smile puts to rest the question whether or not a higher being exists. Only one greater than man could create such precious sights to wandering eyes. May I?"

Just like a gentleman, Das kisses the hand of each lady. Afterwards, he and Kristoffe escorts the dames to the carriage in which the ladies arrived. Soon, the group is on their way to Cristone—a very elegant restaurant, which offers a romantic dining experience for its couples—each getting acquainted with one another.

Upon the well-dressed group's arrival to the restaurant, the two brothers escort the two highly attractive ladies inside. After being seated by the hostess, the group engages conversation. Although Das enjoys himself, his mind is preoccupied by thoughts of Janicah. Periodically, he tunes out everyone's voice and thinks about his new friend. Noticing his brother's short attention span, Kristoffe grabs his brother's attention.

"Brother, are you still with us?"

Das stares blankly as if he doesn't hear the call.

"Das! Are you okay?" Kristoffe asks.

The ladies and Kristoffe quietly stare at Das and await his response. Suddenly, Das realizes his neglect towards the group.

"I apologize, Kristoffe. I was thinking about something. I didn't mean to disrespect any of you. I just haven't been myself lately."

"You haven't been yourself for quite some time, my older brother." Kristoffe jokes with a chuckle.

Jessica smiles then places her hand on Das's lap.

"I'm sure he's a busy man with a busy mind, right Das?"

Das returns the amicable smile to Jessica then slowly removes her hand from his thigh, kissing it twice.

"So right you are my nightly sapphire!"

"Good. Now let's continue with this evening everyone!" Jessica commands with a smirk.

The group again engages in conversation. However, Das falls victim to his periodic thoughts of Janicah throughout the night. Nevertheless, he finds a way to not ruin the evening.

Following a beautiful and fun-filled night of conversation, dinner and dance, the elegant group leaves the restaurant, laughing and giggling to the coach. Once inside, Kristoffe and Monique snuggle close to each other as Jessica tries to be affectionate with Das. Although Das doesn't want to lead Jessica on, he allows her the opportunity to rest her head on his shoulder, feeling compelled to kiss her crown. Surprised, Jessica thanks him with a smile. Thereafter, until the group arrives to Das's and Kristoffe's home, each couple converse in whispers.

When the coach stops in front of the gentlemen's home, Das exits the carriage. Monique, Jessica and Kristoffe follows. While standing next to the coach, Kristoffe kisses Monique while Das gives Jessica a friendly embrace. Suddenly, Kristoffe erupts.

"Ladies, why don't you be so kind and join us for the rest of the evening?"

"I don't know, Kristoffe." Monique hesitates.

"I'm sure they're tired," Das assumes.

"Ladies," Kristoffe continues as he stares seductively into Monique's eyes, "tonight you are in no danger. You are with two gentlemen who will guarantee your safe return home. Monique, if you will, please tell your driver he has no reason to stay."

For a few moments, silence fills the darkness. Monique looks at Jessica who glances at Das.

"What do you think we should do, Das?" Jessica questions.

"The offer has been made by my brother, which is also my invite. If you two would like to be in our company for the remainder of the evening, this smile will only widen."

"Monique," Jessica calls, "I don't see any harm in staying. Tell Vilas he may return in the morning."

Satisfied by her friend's response, Monique orders her coachman to return in the morning. Once he pulls away and disappears into the night, the energetic crowd enters the house.

Upon entry, the ladies and Das sit on the sofa as Kristoffe disappears into the kitchen only to return with a bottle of Montigue d'Apshelle. Carefully, he fills each person's glass then takes a seat next to Monique. Again, the group continues to converse and laugh drunkenly.

After a two-hour session of story-telling, three bottles of wine and drunken debates, Kristoffe and Monique stagger up the stairs, stumbling into Kristoffe's room—leaving Das and Jessica alone. Das shakes his head at his brother's actions then returns his focus to Jessica.

"Das," Jessica whispers while holding Das in front of the fireplace, "tell me why you haven't tried to kiss me all night? Am I not attractive to you?"

"Jessica, although your body and your majestic personality attract me, I'm refraining from acting on my thoughts."

"What do you mean?"

"I'm trying to change my ways. If this same situation were to happen seven months ago, I would've been all over you. Since I'm learning to love a woman's mind prior to yearning for her body, I'll continue to remain a gentleman."

"I find that sweet. Men usually don't care about a woman's mind. They just want that which is between her legs!"

"Not long ago, I was one of those men. Thus, my reason for moving here where I don't know anyone and, no one knows me."

"I see. Well, we haven't known each other long enough for you to love my mind, and you don't want my body, what do you suggest we do?"

"Hold each other and discuss life."

"What about life?"

"I want you to tell me a little about your past, your present and what you wish to achieve in the future. In turn, I will do the same."

"Sounds fair."

Das and Jessica hold each other in front of the fireplace, conversing as if they've known each other for years. Periodically, they're interrupted by Kristoffe's moans and Monique's screams.

"Busy aren't they?" Jessica whispers.

"Yeah," Das sighs, listening to the thumping above, "my brother is quite a specimen."

"They'd dated some time ago, right?"

"They did, off and on, but I'm not sure what happened. I see he cares quite a bit for Monique."

"Funny how time allows love to heal, huh?"

"Time?" Das's eyes focus on the crackling fire before him. "Yeah, it's an interesting factor in a healing process. It's the only thing we have, yet we don't have much of it to lose…"

After a half an hour of talking over Kristoffe's and Monique's night-play, the annoying bellows and outbursts suddenly cease, providing Das and Jessica the opportunity to continue their conversation.

"What do you like most about yourself, Das?"

"I've never been asked that question. I'm embarrassed for I do not know."

"Think hard!"

"I realize my past faults and insecurities, and I like the fact I'm trying to change. I like that I am growing emotionally and spiritually."

"Really? You've undergone a lot in your life, right?"

"All that I've undergone, and all that I have put many through cannot be measured by any man-made instrument."

"That deep huh? Well let's change the subject…"

Partially intoxicated and following a couple hours of pillow talk, the two recently acquainted friends fall asleep in each other's arms.

Fireplace logs now ashes, sunlight peeping through the blinds, Das and Jessica awake to knocking on the door. Still fatigue and affected by the wine, Jessica looks at Das and he looks at her—both yawning and not wanting to be bothered.

"Are you expecting someone, Das?"

"I believe that may be your coachman."

"That's right. What time is it?"

"A little after eleven," Das utters while focusing on the grandfather clock.

Very slowly while trying to maintain his balance, Das stands to his feet then sways drunkenly to the door. Jessica searches frantically for her shoes. Once she has them in her hands, Das slowly opens the door.

"Bonjour Monsieur. I come for Monique and Jessica."

"Indeed. I will have the ladies at your coach momentarily," Das assures.

"Bon! *(good)* I shall wait for them next to the coach."

As Das watches as Vilas return to his carriage, Jessica approaches him, giving him a fond embrace.

"I think I should go and get my friend."

"Sit for a moment," Das smiles, "I'll return with both her and my brother."

Das kisses Jessica on the cheek then hurries up the stairs. Respectfully, he knocks on his brother's door.

"Who is it?" Kristoffe bellows.

"Brother, Vilas, the ladies' coachman, has arrived."

"What time is it?"

"Time for Monique and Jessica to leave!"

"I'll be out in a moment, Das." Monique cackles as if she's being tickled.

"Good. Jessica and I will be downstairs waiting for you."

Das joins Jessica on the couch where they wait for Kristoffe and Monique. After fifteen minutes of waiting, the two giggle as they watch Monique nearly tumble down the steps. "That's not funny," she blurts. Das continues to smile.

Robe open, chest showing, Kristoffe follows closely behind Monique.

"Like I said ladies," Kristoffe utters, "we've caused you no harm."

"Speak for yourself, Kristoffe," Monique responds with a smile of grief, "I'll need to soak for quite some time when I get home due to your rough-housing. Nevertheless, last night will forever be remembered."

"I'm sure," Kristoffe gloats. "My ability to please a woman is definitely a God-given gift."

"Don't get too full of yourself, Kristoffe." Das interjects.

Jessica and Das watch as Monique pigeon-steps toward them. The expression of soreness jogs across her face as she accomplishes each step. With a concerned smile, Jessica and Das look at each other then burst into laughter.

"What's so funny?" Monique asks.

"He must've really did some work on you," Jessica chuckles.

"That he did. Now let's go before Vilas grows upset."

Like the gentlemen they are, Kristoffe and Das escort the ladies to their coach, each holding hands with his partner. Following a series of hugs, kisses and thank yous, Das and Kristoffe watch as the coach becomes an image in the rising noon's sun.

"So how was your night, Kristoffe?"

"Didn't you hear us? I was planting memories into Monique."

"Planting memories?"

"Yes! She will not forget the night that Kristoffe gave her two orgasms and her uncomfortable walk. Each time she think about last night, her yearn for me will grow."

"Possibly, yet, it may all be forgotten when some one gives her three or more orgasms and causes her to crawl for relief." Das smirks.

While discussing matters pertaining to the night previous, Das and Kristoffe reenter their home, continuing their conversation on the couch. Afterwards, like so many times before, the two go about the day as they individually choose.

Happily for the next few days, Das and Kristoffe continue to spend time with Monique and Jessica. Each day the four venture through the park and enjoy one another's company. However, Das continues to think about Janicah. Each night following the days he spends with Jessica, he wanders whether or not he'll hear from Janicah again. Sadly, as the days continue to go by, Das begins to withdraw himself from Jessica for he believes that he is meant for a woman he does not know—Janicah.

Now as thoughts of Janicah occupy Das's mind, thoughts of him occupy hers also. In addition to her daily activities, Janicah looks forward to receiving Das's letter. Each night she prays and believes he is a Godsend, and each morning she tries to predict the delivery of his letter.

Assuming that Das had sent his letter the same day of receiving hers, Janicah concludes she is to receive his correspondence in six or seven days. Thus, she continues her day-to-day activities and waits, impatiently.

On the sixth day Janicah believes to receive word from Das, she doesn't. Surprisingly, Chati doesn't stop by at all. Without worry, Janicah proceeds to fill her day with walking the rues as she looks forward to the day following.

On the seventh morning, Janicah wakes up early and waits impatiently on the living room couch for Chati. She stares out the window and anticipates his arrival with Das's letter. Seven o'clock passes—so does eight. Soon it is noon. At one o'clock, Janicah runs up the stairs and sulks on her bed, heart heavy for she believes Das has chosen not to write her. Saddened by her thought, the possibility of Chati being sick or any other factor that would delay Das's message never crosses her mind. Nevertheless, she becomes slightly hostile—beating her pillow and uttering profanity.

After a few minutes of pounding her pillow and muttering words unbecoming of a lady, Janicah gets dressed then walks her daily course near the ocean. Sadness walks with her as she tries to understand her feelings for a man she has never met. As she looks at the ripples in the ocean, she sits on a rock and realizes that her emotions have gotten the best of her. While staring at the gold and blue sky, she whispers.

> "Never before I have felt so strongly for someone who
> I've known only by words and not by actions or sight—
> All my life I've been made to believe that my happiness
> is to be found within a man's love—this isn't right.
> While I sit here, adhering to my emotions, the ocean
> calms and sooths me as if I'm its child—
> I've allowed myself to feel more than what I should;
> however, I will do as I have prior to finding this man's
> letter—live proud."

After sitting and looking at the ocean, Janicah rises to her feet then completes her stroll. Once she arrives home, she and her mother converse.

"Daughter, why the long face?"

"I haven't received a letter from Das."

"And this causes you to frown. Child, there are many more men out there. Do not let this one whom you've never met cause you this amount of anxiety. How long has it been anyway?"

"Seven days."

"Only seven days? Still you worry? You act as if the world depends on you, but Flower, it doesn't. Give him time—at least another couple of days. It's possible that something could've happened. Who knows? Don't automatically assume he didn't write you."

"You're right. Say, why don't we have a mother and daughter day?"

"What do you have in mind?"

"I say you and I take a trip to the market, come home, and then, talk about life following dinner."

"Sounds good. Let me ready myself."

"I'll wait for you down here."

Janicah's mother struggles up the stairs then preps herself for a day with her daughter. Janicah waits patiently on the couch and thinks about Das. Yet, within a matter of minutes, Janicah's mother hobbles down the stairs. Upon reaching the base of the staircase, she is met by Janicah. Together, the two Santa Lucian belles escort each other to their coach.

As planned, the mother and daughter spend the whole day together, visiting the market, talking about memories past and listening to the band playing in the park. After a fun-filled day together, the ladies return home where they eat dinner, converse and then end the day with card play and conversation.

"Mother."

"Yes, Daughter."

"What is love?"

"I find this question quite humorous for you have never asked it before. When you were involved with Tomus, I thought you knew the answer to that question."

"I was only infatuated with his physique."

"Tell me no more. Nicah, love is a word that many women know and very few men acknowledge. It's pain. It's joy. It's the feeling of never wanting to be away and the feeling of not ever coming back.

Child, love is nothing more than a pleasurable burden meant to be carried by two people."

"So wise you are, Mother…"

Early the next morning, Janicah wakes up to pounding on the front door. Agitated by being disturbed, she gradually stands up then mopes down the stairs. Prior to opening the door, she glances at the clock. It's a quarter to eight. While rubbing her eyes and yawning, she slowly opens the door. Chati stands before her with a huge grin on his face.

"Good morning, young Janicah."

"What's so good about it, Monsieur Chati?"

"We both are alive."

"True. Where were you yesterday?"

"If there's no mail to deliver, there's nothing for me to deliver."

"I see. Even if that's the case, you would usually come and visit for a few moments."

"True that is, but I had much to do yesterday. What's wrong?"

"Nothing really, just tired."

"Very well, let's make this short."

"Good. So what do you have for me or my mother?"

"For your mother—nothing, but for you, this."

Chati hands Janicah an envelope from Das. A smile appears on her face and her tone transforms to excitement.

"Monsieur Chati, you've been forgiven."

"I wasn't aware that I did anything wrong! Were you upset with me for some reason?"

"Not at all."

"Very well, be sure to have a good day, young lady. And tell your mother that I will see her soon."

Janicah's mother tiptoes down the stairs then positions herself behind her daughter. Following a kiss to the back of Janicah's head, she speaks with Chati.

"Denmon Chati. What is it that my daughter should tell me?"

"Good morning, Claire. How are you doing this morning?"

"Age has a funny way of telling the body it is old. Other than the pains in my knees, I'm doing well."

"You're looking well, too!"

"Thank you."

"Claire, why don't you and I go out sometime?"

"I suppose this is the information my daughter was asked to tell me. Like I've told you many times, Denmon, I have no reason to be out and about unless it's with my daughter or one of my friends."

"After all these years, Claire, I thought I was considered your friend…"

Janicah grows tired of listening to her mother and Chati discuss matters which don't pertain to her. She excuses herself from the conversation crossfire then flees to her bedroom, laying on her bed giggling as she reads Das's letter. Freed from tiredness, she grabs her notebook then responds to the man who she thought had forgotten her.

She Answers

> "I smile at your willingness, your compassion and
> your ambition to seek me; not once have you asked my
> age—
> Nor have you asked if I've borne offspring, which tells
> me these are factors not important to you at this stage.
> I am honored, actually, I'm quite pleased that a man
> who haven't seen a woman's face desires her virtue—
> I've asked my sweet Lord to have you respond, and
> if you did, I would care not about your looks or your
> economic status. Each time I read your letter, a warm
> feeling fills me as if I'm covered by a soft, sun kissed
> cloth—
> Your words are not of any man's I've heard before, and
> you're much too sincere to be a façade.
> Since your first letter, I've dreamt of riding on horses as
> the soft winds push my blouse, and behind me a man—
> A man unlike any other, whose face was bronze and
> his hair of wool; nonetheless, one touch made my toes
> curl and my hair stand. Each of his words had its own
> definition; each kiss sent goose bumps down my back
> and caused my clitoris to tickle—

Whenever I awake from this dream, I'm drenched
in sweat; yet I look forward to the night next for the
encore.To your question of my whereabouts, I reside
near the ocean which holds the tourist attraction
Chateau Montelle—
On a pasture with my mother, at the end of the dirt road,
which is the only one close to the cliffs. Let me know
when you plan to arrive for I will ready a room and
have fun-filled events ready for my guest—
In addition to these words is a kiss from my lips and
a rose petal that I request you treat as if they were
valuable gifts.

Farewell, Janicah"

After writing her letter, Janicah tosses it onto her desk, jumps
to her feet and then gathers her clothes for the day. Afterwards, she
prances into the bathroom where she readies a bath and unties her
hair. While looking in the mirror, she smiles at her reflection as she
disrobes. Next, one foot after the other, she enters the tub, adapting
to the muscle relaxing-water. Aroused by erotic thoughts of Das, she
pleases herself while whispering.

"Kind is the man whose words can bring trembles to a
woman's body and not make her feel weaker than he—
While many are with selfishness and greed, he seems
to be different; nevertheless, he brings weakness to my
knees. How deep will my love be for this man as time
continues and prepare me for our acquaintance—
Strong in heart and mind I am; yet, feeble I'll be for a
man who can want me without knowing my touch or
appearance."

Moments upon pleasing herself, Janicah finish her bath then
wrap a towel around her naked torso. Afterwards, she enters her
room and jumps onto the bed. Following a brief thought about her
day, she gets dressed. After snatching her letter, she rushes down the
stairs and dashes into the living room where her mother and Chati
continue to talk.

"Monsieur Chati, I see you're still here," Janicah utters as if surprised.

"That I am," Chati smiles. "Your mother and I were just speaking of memories past."

"Really? What memories do you and my mother hold secret?"

Janicah's mother places a finger on Chati's lips then focuses her attention on her daughter.

"Daughter, do not ask questions that require lengthy answers. Tell me. Did you receive a letter from your friend?"

"Yes, I did."

"What is in your hand?"

"My reply to him."

Janicah advances towards Chati then hands him the envelope.

"Monsieur Chati, deliver this as if your life depends on it!"

Janicah's mother chuckles as Chati smiles goofily at Janicah.

"Once I deliver this to the mail station, Janicah," Chati utters, "it's out of my hands. If something were to happen to it—it wouldn't be my fault."

"Well, from now until you reach the station, treat it as if it has some importance to you."

"Will do."

Janicah kisses her mother on the cheek then exits the house. Like many days before, she strolls along the ocean while thinking about Das as she continues her routine.

During Das's anticipation of Janicah's response, he and Kristoffe experience complications with one another. Unknowingly, Das's decision to no longer see Jessica causes problems between Kristoffe and Monique. One day at the park, Monique tells Kristoffe of Jessica's request for her to not see him anymore.

"Kristoffe," Monique sighs while staring into his eyes, "it is unfortunate that I tell you this."

"Tell me what?"

"It is Jessica's wish for you and I to no longer see each other!"

"Why?" Kristoffe asks frantically.

"Well, since Das chooses to no longer see Jessica, it is best that we no longer see each other as well. I'm awfully sorry!"

"Sorry? What is it that you're sorry for? I give you my heart and you the audacity to let your friend control you!"

"What's done is done! I'm just sorry. I pray you can forgive me."

Monique kisses Kristoffe on the forehead, leaving him sitting alone on a bench. Once she enters her carriage and disappears into the day, rage fills Kristoffe. Driven by loath for his brother, Kristoffe saddles his horse and hurries home. Angry and appalled from what he was told, Kristoffe bursts through the door.

"Das, where are you?"

To Kristoffe's yell, Das quickly leaves his room then runs down the stairs only to be met by frowns and snarls.

"Kristoffe! What is this?"

"Damn you, Das!"

Startled by his brother's expression, Das takes a step back.

"Damn me? Why?"

Kristoffe advances towards Das then stares into his eyes.

"My words aren't foreign to you, are they brother? Why do I say damn you—you ask? I'll be happy to tell you. Your reason to not see Jessica has become a barrier between Monique and me."

"Don't blame me for your inability to please a woman, Kristoffe!"

Like a zephyr against leaves, Das blows by Kristoffe then takes a seat in his chair. Kristoffe quickly follows.

"Don't ever turn your back on me again, Das!"

"Kristoffe, sit and talk to me as if you have an ounce of respect. I refuse to join you in this heated discussion. If you want me to listen and converse in a fashion suitable for gentlemen, you must change your tone!"

Kristoffe sits on the sofa then takes a deep breath. Shortly after, he continues in a less agitated fashion.

"Das, I've always liked Monique, and I thought I would never see her again. This is a chance for me to make things right."

Das chuckles silently while staring at his brother.

"Kristoffe, you've never truly cared about a woman before, so why now? To you, a woman is nothing but a play toy."

"My thinking of a woman's place and duties haven't change; however, I can see myself with Monique."

"You must not be that important to her if she's choosing her friend over you."

"Enough! Are you going to go out with Jessica—or not?"

"For what reason—your convenience? I have no intentions of wanting to be with Jessica. If Monique chooses to use this as her ploy to rid you from her life, she is the one you must confront—not me!"

"What happened to you? You were once a man I admired. Some how, you've evolved into another whom I don't know. Is your unwillingness to court Jessica due to your Santa Lucia harlot?"

"Hold your tongue, Kristoffe!"

"No! You hold your tongue, Das. I'm tired of living here with a man who I thought was my brother. I see now, I'm with a stranger!"

Kristoffe leaps from the sofa, challenging his brother to stand. Das hesitantly accepts the invite and looks directly into his brother's eyes.

"Kristoffe, although your anger for me can be justified, I beseech you to back away from me."

"And if I don't?"

"Is this lady so important that you're willing to fight me?"

"My fighting you wouldn't be over Monique—it would be due to my lost of patience and respect for you."

"Brother, I do not wish to quarrel, so please move."

Das places a hand on Kristoffe's shoulder, pushing him aside gently. Irate at his brother's insincere actions, Kristoffe shoves Das into the wall, sending Das's favorite painting crashing to the floor. After regaining his balance, Das stares sadly at his ruined painting of Chia Monte—a nude, dark woman surrounded by specs of light. Following a slow, controlled blink, a tear falls from the cliff of Das's right eyelashes. Partially upset, he focuses his attention on the culprit.

"I've come here to Dalay to escape my violent behavior and indecent ways," Das reasons. "Yet, I wasn't aware of my bringing the catalyst, which would make me act in the fashion I've tried so hard to abandon. I can fight you, but what would that prove? Nothing. Before I do something, which is beneath me, I'm retiring to my room. Have a pleasant day, Kristoffe!"

Das picks up his painting then adjourns to his room. Kristoffe slams the door then pounces on the sofa.

While Das sits and weeps on his bed, an anger he thought he had buried hovers over him like an autumn cloud over a city. Nevertheless, instead of acting on his thoughts to tussle with his younger brother, he writes in his journal until night falls. Sadly, neither brother speaks to the other.

Early the next morning, Kristoffe awakes to knocking on the door. Agitated, he slowly sits up, slides on his slippers then stomps down the stairs. When he opens the door, he growls.

"Justin, what do you have for Das?"

"I see someone is not happy this fine morning."

"You're here to deliver something, right? Well deliver it!"

"It's obvious you're having issues. If my coming here at this time is a bother to you, I'll leave the mail on the steps. How does that sound?"

"Do as you must."

Justin hands two envelopes to Kristoffe. One is Janicah's letter to Das, and the other is from Amecca, the eldest sister of the two brothers. As Kristoffe reads the letter from Amecca, he carefully climbs the stairs then reluctantly enters his brother's room.

"Das!"

Das peeps from the cubbyhole of his blankets.

"I don't want to argue with you, Kristoffe," Das grumbles.

"That's good for I didn't come here to argue, Das!"

"What is it then?"

"Your mystery lady from Santa Lucia has sent word to you."

Das pops up from his blanket wad like a dolphin leaping for its dinner.

"Give it to me."

"Certainly."

Kristoffe hands Das Janicah's letter then shows him the letter from Amecca.

"Amecca has written us also. I see you're not as excited to get a letter from your family; yet, you grow excited to know a woman whom you do not know writes you. I tell you—you're very interesting."

"What does Amecca say?"

"Nothing really—just that she wishes for us to visit."

"I see. Perhaps that's possible. Now if you may, please excuse me."

Kristoffe flees from his brother's room then rushes into his own. Alone and happy to receive word from Janicah, Das opens the envelope then begins reading. Smiles trample his face as he completes each line. Once finished, he sits at his desk then writes to his eloquent, mystery lady.

He Speaks

> "My fair lady, I do not need to know your age because
> your words alone speak of wisdom and maturity—
> Words of those you speak tell me that you are a Merlot,
> perfectly aged for a divine taste, so sweet.
> In the heat of my joys, I perspire with anticipation as I
> think of meeting you and learning your mind—
> For so long time has been my enemy; yet it has given
> me reason to smile and leave all my afflictions behind.
> I know my wanting to see you is odd, but this desire to
> meet your acquaintance overwhelms my curiosity—
> Surely, my family will consider me foolish if I were
> to leave on a whim; however, to see you is a quest I
> must defeat. You can expect me possibly a day or two
> following your receiving this letter in your soft, gentle
> hands—
> I believe I have become the man that I dreamt to be;
> nevertheless, this is due to your majestic words and
> God's plan.
> Is it possible that a dream can become reality? I
> truly believe all that I thought was impossible is now
> improbable—

Can it be a dream is reality? I truly believe that I can
make all of which I thought was improbable the
possible.

See you soon—Das Treymone"

Das folds the letter then slides it carefully into an envelope.
Following a sigh, he calls to his brother.

"Kristoffe!"

After waiting a few moments, Das yells his brother's name
again. This time louder than before.

"Kristoffe, come here!"

Very grumpily, Kristoffe yells from his room.

"What is it?"

"Come here!"

Kristoffe stomps toward Das's room. Arms folded, he leans
against Das's bedroom entranceway.

"What do you want, Das?"

"Let's not be upset with each other any longer."

"You got me out of bed for that?"

"I have something else to tell you."

"I'm waiting."

Das sighs. Next he braces himself as he tells Kristoffe about his
leaving.

"Before I say anything, I want to let you know that I love you
dearly."

"Go on!"

"You may find this silly, but I'm leaving for Santa Lucia in a
couple of days."

Kristoffe stands baffled. Disgust crawls across his face as he
strategically positions himself nearly two feet from his brother.
Outrage fills his lips.

"You bring me out here then leave! How dare you put your lips
together to say something so atrocious?"

"Kristoffe, I appreciate your coming to Dalay with me, and I
will never forget your good deed. However, I never told you once
that you had to stay. If it makes you feel any better, I promise to
return shortly."

28

"What am I to do while you're visiting a woman whom you have not seen?"

"You're an adult! Visit Amecca and the rest of the family. You're no prisoner here!"

"Neither Amecca nor the rest of the family will be happy with your decision."

"I'm willing to live with everyone's dissatisfaction in order to find my own satisfaction."

"You know something, Das. You're a self-centered bastard!"

"How is that when I sacrificed so much for you, Amecca, Missilia and De Ano? If anything, I've been probably more gracious then I should've been. If you don't mind, I have some packing and planning to do. By the way, are you going in to town?"

Kristoffe frowns and continues to stare at his brother.

"Perhaps. Why?"

"Could you be so kind to take this to the mail station?"

"No—not this time, brother!"

"Very well. I'll do it myself. Your presence is no longer needed, so please leave!"

Kristoffe slowly backs out of his brother's room. His eyes fill with tears. His heart pounds nervously as he hurries to his room. The slamming of his bedroom door forces Das to realize the pain he has caused. However, as Das thinks about all that he had done and sacrificed for his family, a single tear slides down his face, stopping at the corner of his lips. Although slightly agitated and hurt, he gets dressed then leaves the house.

After mounting his horse, Das rides to the mail station where he ensures the delivery of his letter. Upon his return home, he notices that Kristoffe has abandoned the premises. Feeling no need to worry, and motivated by thoughts of Janicah, he hurries to his room where he prepares his luggage and writes in his journal. Unfortunately, for that night and the one following, Kristoffe doesn't return home.

2
The Quest

Early the next morning that Das had planned to leave, Kristoffe enters the house, reeking of perfume and liquor. At the top of his lungs, he yells his brother's name.

"Das!"

Das leaves his room with his luggage then gallop down the stairs. Eye-to-eye with his brother, he sees the displeased expression on Kristoffe's face. Slowly, he shuffles by him then takes a seat on the sofa. Kristoffe follows and sits in the chair adjacent to him.

"Did you have fun, Kristoffe?"

"I did."

"Where have you been and what did you do?"

"I went everywhere I pleased and did all of which was my business."

"I see."

"So do you need a ride to the train station—brother?"

"It will be greatly appreciated."

"And if I wouldn't have returned, what would you have done?"

"I knew you would return for you would like me to be happy."

"This woman! What if she is not the woman you've pictured?"

"If she is even slightly different from what her words suggest, I shall return at once. Now, if we're done discussing the matter at hand, I suggest you go bathe. Afterwards, you and I can discuss anything on your mind."

"I have nothing else to discuss with you. Once I return from my bath, I'll take you to the train station!"

"Thank you, Kristoffe."

"Don't thank me!"

Kristoffe turns away quickly then dashes up the stairs, stomping into his room. He then runs into the bathroom. As he freshens himself, Das waits patiently on the sofa. Although he blames himself for his brother's frustration, excitement storms his mind as he thinks about Janicah. And after each hypnotizing moment thinking about his destiny, he smiles.

After finishing his hygiene, Kristoffe stomps angrily down the stairs, awakening his brother from his daze. From the base of the staircase, he stares with fury at his brother.

"By what time do you need to be at the train station?"

"Your timing couldn't be more perfect," Das voices as he looks at the clock. "It's ten now, so within a few minutes, we should leave."

"Have you reconsidered your decision?" Kristoffe asks as anger still inflames his voice.

"No. There's no reason to do so."

"So you say!"

Kristoffe mopes into the living room then takes a seat next to his brother; yet he says nothing. Das, on the other hand, turns his focus to his angered and agitated sibling.

"I left the address to where I'll be in the kitchen. If an emergency should arise, don't hesitate to send for me."

Kristoffe replies with a sigh. Afterwards, he nods.

Following the pass of a few, silent minutes, the time for Das to leave is at hand.

"Let's go, Kristoffe. My destiny awaits me."

"Are you sure you want to go?"

"I've never been surer of anything else."

"Very well, let's go."

The two brothers exit the house then mount their three-horse carriage. In a matter of moments, they head towards the train station.

During the thirty-minute journey, neither Das nor Kristoffe say anything. Each man wrestles with his own thoughts. Das tangles with his thoughts of Janicah while Kristoffe tries to defeat his own thoughts of cursing his brother. Yet, upon their arrival at the train station, the two dismount the carriage then stroll toward the waiting area.

"Kristoffe, I assume you're not going to say anything to me, right?"

Kristoffe droops his head toward the ground. His eyes slowly close.

"Your silence answers my question," Das affirms sadly.

Kristoffe raises his head then focuses his attention on his brother.

"Das, I'm aware that my actions are less than desired by you, but you must understand how I feel. I left my job and my lifestyle to ensure your well-being. Now, after a couple of letters from a woman whom you do not know, you're leaving me. I find that very inconsiderate and very disrespectful."

"Now that I look at it, Kristoffe, my actions are and were rather impious. For this, I apologize for the grief and anguish I've caused you. Although you left your job for my sake, money has never been an issue. To say the least, I have given you all you need to live any lifestyle that you so desire."

Kristoffe smiles then wraps an arm around his brother's back.

"Apology accepted. Das, what I am about to say to you must not be repeated or discussed with anyone, alright?"

"Have I ever uttered your secrets?"

"Yes, you have. Remember when I told you I put snails in Amecca's soup and you promised that you wouldn't tell?"

"Yeah," Das laughs, "that was amusing!"

"When you told, I was the person blamed for her vomiting."

"That was different. We're adults now. You can speak all that is on your mind to me."

"Good. Honestly, I've always been envied and admired by your ability to be so decisive. You've always gone for what you wanted and didn't let anything stop you."

"It doesn't happen much, Kristoffe. Believe it or not, this is the first in some time now."

The two brother's conversation comes to an end as the train howls afar off in the distance. With smiles on their faces, the two brothers give each other a hug.

"This is it, Kristoffe."

"That it is, Das."

Shortly following the train's ear-deafening, screeching halt, and the operator's "All aboard to Santa Lucia" bellow, Das joins the boarding passengers. Once seated, he smiles from the window and waves. Kristoffe returns the amicable gestures until the train disappears into the day. When he can no longer see the train,

Kristoffe releases a single tear then struggles to the coach. Before he leaves the train station, he whispers a prayer for his brother's safety.

"Lord I know I haven't talked to you in quite some time; however, I need you to do me a favor. Bless the path that my brother has chosen to follow. Allow him a safe passage towards his destiny. Protect him! Shield him! Forgive him for he sometimes does not understand what he often does. He follows his heart and leads with his mind; therefore, enter his heart and become his mind. In Your name I pray, Amen!"

After his prayer, Kristoffe heads home.

Following six days and five nights of travel, Das arrives to Santa Lucia. After exiting the train, he walks forward a few feet then stops for a moment to appreciate the city's dark beauty. The wind welcomes him with a subtle touch while the night's sun illumes proudly from the sleeping heavens above. Upon taking a moment to welcome the foreign area, Das shuffles toward a tall, dark-skinned coachman standing next to a beautiful white and red stagecoach.

"Good day Sir, are you available?"

"Yes I am. To where would you like me to take you this evening?"

Das pulls Janicah's address and the directions to her home from his wallet then hands it to the coachman. After viewing the sheet, the coachman smiles.

"Oh yes, the Mi'Voir residence. I know exactly where that is."

"Will it take long for us to arrive?"

"It's a small journey so we'll be there in no time."

"Thank you."

Das boards the carriage then rests his head against the window. Once the coach sets in motion, he falls asleep.

In less than twenty minutes, Das awakes to the carriage's sudden stop. Before he regains coherency, the coachman slowly opens the door.

"We have arrived, sir."

Das looks around. A calm darkness surrounds the carriage. Yet, a small light shines from the house before him. Still, somewhat lethargic, he carefully exits the coach.

"Thank you, young man," Das whispers.

"It was my pleasure."

Following his tip to the coachman and the coachman's departure, Das steps toward the house. Suddenly, a familiar joy fills him, which wards off his tiredness. With confidence, he knocks twice on the door, and then takes a step back. Within moments, Janicah's mother opens the door.

"Hello Monsieur. How may I help you?"

"Forgive my late disturbance, Madame, but I seek Janicah Mi'Voir."

"I'm her mother, Claire. Let me guess. You must be Das, right?"

"Indeed I am."

Claire's matured beauty baffles Das. Although she's three months shy of fifty-seven, she appears to be only thirty. Das clears his throat, but before he could say another word, Janicah approaches her mother from the rear. Das's eyes glisten at the mocha-skinned young lady with hazel eyes. Janicah, too, marvels at the deep brown-skinned man slightly quivering before her.

"Well, I see my place is in my room," Claire smiles. "I'll leave you two young folks alone."

"Mother, is there anything you would like me to do for you?"

"Child, no! You have company. I'll be upstairs if you need me."

Claire smiles at Das once again.

"I don't have to worry about my daughter, do I young man?"

"Madame, I shall be respectful of you, your house and your daughter."

"Good. Well that's my cue to leave. Goodnight children."

"Goodnight, mama!"

Shortly following Claire's absence, Janicah invites Das into her home then leads him to an aged, burgundy sofa. While sitting next to each other, Janicah kisses Das's left hand then rekindles conversation.

> "My Lord have planted me as a seed to grow—to
> become what? I did not know until this moment—
> As I touch your hand, I am happy to see that you're
> more beautiful than the vision I've been holding.

I ask that you grant me the permission to allow the
resting of my head on your chest—
And to think of me as an orphan who wishes to be held
like a child to its mother's breast."

He Speaks

"I want you to enter my mind and walk the destitute
path towards a heart which knows no laughs—
Which knows no joys and no smiles, and no sun in a
day nor knows of any stars that shine in the night.
Don't ask me to grant you permission, for your wish
shall be granted once asked—
So long I've been burdened with doubt; now that I am
here, I can finally say free at last."

Janicah rests her head against Das's cologne-scented chest.
Afterwards, she takes a deep breath then exhales slowly.

She Answers

"What captures my attention is to know that
imagination has no limitations, no shackles or braces—
Although similar to many hypocrites, it doesn't get to
choose its array of faces.
For so long, I've imagined growing alone and old only
to gain sovereignty over my regrets and anguish—
To finally extinguish the flames fueled by life's
disappointments and this world's selfishness.
How was your journey? I hope it welcomed you as I
did; nevertheless, I'm sure it was long and wearisome—
Speak to me about your life ails and heated quarrels so I
can really understand you more clearly."

Janicah continues to stare wondrously at Das; Das's eyes shift
toward the living room's wooden floor. He, then, closes his eyes and
responds.

Ellard Thomas

He Speaks

> "Such a story may take days, perhaps months, but all
> I know is that it has no conclusion, just the effects of
> suffering—
> I remember as a young child I had everything—a
> mother, siblings and never was I with nothing."

Janicah interrupts. Yet, Das doesn't get upset. Instead, he forces himself to smile.

She Answers

> "I know your memories are with many complications,
> and I know from experience that the past is a path we
> do not wish to travel—
> Nevertheless, it reminds us to remember that we are
> soldiers in life's army; still we must not ever forget our
> battles.
> My desire is to know your past so I can show you a
> future that is fit only for a man like you—
> I beg that you not feel uptight or get upset for my
> wanting to know your past will help my getting to know
> you."

Das looks into Janicah's eyes as his own fill with tears of sorrow. Although he wishes to turn away, he's fixated on Janicah. Sadly, tears from thinking about his past skates down his face. After a few gather at the corner of his lips, Janicah wipes them away with the sleeve of her summer dress. Das clears his throat and continues.

> "Does the sun shine for everyone who plays in green
> pastures and those whom stroll in the rues, but exclude
> me? When the heavens cry only to bring beauty to all
> of which have been scorched by a summer's breath,
> should I not grow like the weeds?
> Long ago I knew of a light that was so beautiful and
> more glamorous than the sun, which the world called
> woman, but I called mother—

36

As a young child I had many riches and knew no such
conditions as poverty, homelessness, violence and
molestation, and never had to suffer.
My mother worked hard to ensure I had all that I
wanted and needed for I was her only child at fifteen—
Although she was merely a child who knew no
direction, she was certain that a man in her life would
make her feel like a queen."

Das stops for a moment to take a breath. Tears trample down his
cheeks and fall onto Janicah's head. As he weeps, she weeps as well.
Wiping away his tears, Das continues.

"I recall it was a Sunday of gloom when no moonlight
escaped from the dark night nor stars saw fit to
flicker—
That day my mother pranced happily into the house
with an extremely dark fellow who greeted me with
a smile, and then, a snicker. Being six-foot-three, he
stood enormously above my four-foot frame; however,
I did not feel scared or even afraid—
That day I was no longer a bastard's child for I had
someone to call father; nevertheless, my bright hopes
would soon turn gray. Once my mother introduced him
to Papa, her grandfather, she was quickly told of his
disapproval—
Sadly, it was that day which marked my journey of
sadness, and it was that day which ended the life that I
was use to.
At the beginning, I felt no harsh vibe for this man
probably because I was excited to have a father figure
in my life—
Unfortunately, I was naive and possibly ignorant, but I
only wanted to be a child who would grow up right.
Initially, he seemed very nice as he accepted my two-
year younger sister, Amecca and me as if we were his—
Time has a funny way of revealing the true face behind
a façade, and it did when I first witnessed him strike

my mother's lips. I dare not say his name now, but my
mother use to call him Cheetah; yet if I had the choice I
would've called him coward—
For years I've grown under his indecent ways; sadly, all
that I've encountered has allowed hate and denial to be
my only sources of power..."

As Das continues to speak, his once clear tone turns into slight
murmurs. Thinking about his past arouses great emotions that he
has held in for so long. Filled with sympathy, Janicah brings her
disturbed friend's head to her bosom like a mother consoling her
child.

She Answers

"I feel I am to blame for your weeping for it was I who
asked you to share with me your pained past—
I meant no harm in my asking, yet, from your tears that
flow from your eyes, I should've never asked.
I see the dawn creeping; therefore, it is best that you
rest easy so we can smile at the arrival of a new day—
If you would like to finish your story, I will listen and
try to not interrupt you as I have done twice today.
Although you're with pain and hurt, I can see the shine
in your spirit like the new fallen snow glistens—
If we are to be as one in the future, making you happy
and helping you smile will be my lifelong mission.
At this moment, I'm wishing your pain were mine
to bear for I want you to be free from agony and
anguish—
In your path will be a bright future that will end
your suffering, which will soon have your sadness
languished."

Das takes a deep breath then exhales slowly. Thereafter, he
continues his story.

He Speaks

"It was in Savia where I was permitted to see certain
things I shouldn't have, like my mother abused for the
first time—
At thirteen I didn't possess the strength to fight
Cheetah, and even after being beat, my mother stayed
with him, still I ask why. For two years this continued,
yet, it must have been God's order to have my mother
uproot us from Savia to live with her mother in Mal—
It was there I enjoyed a life that was only familiar to me
when I was a young, innocent and naïve child.
Over a course of six months, my family and I no longer
lived dysfunctional; we lived a normal life like real
children—
During that time spent with my family and having fun,
happiness was not a hope, it was an actual feeling.
One unfortunate day, Cheetah arrived at my
grandmother's house, pleading and begging for my
mother to return with him—
As I watched him kneel before her, I prayed that she
would laugh in his face then immediately kick and hit
him.
Soon the happiness that I knew so well became a
memory because my mother believed Cheetah's terrible
act and promises—
As I think about that day, Janicah, the whole thought
makes me want to run to the latrine, sulk on my knees
and vomit…"

While telling his story, Das's day of gloom plays in his mind
similar to a recorder with no way of shutting off. He vividly
remembers Cheetah walking from a two horse-driven coach to Das's
grandmother's house. Das can hear his child self yell, "Go away!" to
Cheetah. Afterwards, he runs into the house. The commotion lures
Das's mother from inside of the brick home. Upon stepping foot
onto the porch, her eyes widen at her dark, well-dressed lover. After
conversing with Cheetah for a few moments, Das's mother packs

the children's clothes, kisses her mother on the cheek and then goes off with Cheetah to reside in Savia.

Upon the family's return, Das's mother continues to get abused for the next three years. Fed up with Cheetah's mistreating of her and her kids, she leaves again. Fortunately, the thought of her children being in harm's way makes her realize the importance of life. Das explains to Janicah that his freedom from abuse, neglect and horrid sights was shortly lived.

Das finishes his story. Janicah remains silent. Once her thoughts are well formulated, she responds.

She Answers

>"By the way you speak about this memory, I sense there
>is a lot of resentment towards your mother, but your
>hate is toward Cheetah—
>All that you have gone through has made you stronger
>than many; nevertheless, let's try to leave these issues
>in Savia."

He Speaks

>"My lady, my mind is frail and I shall not go into
>great depths with winded events and stories about my
>dysfunctional life—
>To sum up this anger, I became a sexually abused child
>because of Cheetah's cousin sneaking into my room
>when I was two years beyond five.
>The result of being beat by Cheetah's fist is a child
>whose only want was to live as a child who instead
>became a piñata—
>In short, I'm a sibling to a molested sister, a son of a
>battered mother and the first bastard of a man named
>Don.
>As the years passed, I became the oldest of five siblings
>that God gave me strength to take care of and provide
>care for—

Fraternal twins De Ano and Misilia, my sister Amecca,
and my brother Kristoffe who all helped strengthen me
for this life's war.
My fair Janicah, a childhood I was entitled to was taken
away by the man who I've called father for over nine
years—
My tears no longer come from the sadness of my past,
but the uncertainty of what my future holds near.
Is it death without revenge, a life's sentence in prison
with my thoughts of loneliness, or is it to live life with
you?
I want life for I have experienced death, but what I have
is the memories of a child who was separated from his
family and his virtue…"

Das's voice withers as he grows closer and closer to exhaustion.
Janicah continues to stroke his wavy, black hair.

She Answers

"I've asked God for a cobblestone, yet, He in turn
has sent me a gem, and for a mate, He has sent me an
angel—
Within you is more beauty and wander than there are
colors and rays that are found within the body of a
rainbow. It is by God's grace that I am allowed to hold
you, kiss your face and feel all the pains that you do—
It is God who has solved my mystery and completed
my puzzle when all I asked for was a sign or a clue.
My prince, please sleep for you no longer shall weep
alone for this day is the day you and I set foot onto our
trail—
I promise to be here with you whether I'm approached
by adversity, others' thoughts of me, or sentenced to
Satan's jail. Sleep well, my love, for I'll pray that your
dreams embark upon you all of your truest desires and
best wishes—

41

Tomorrow will be the day when you and I will talk
further, but for now, I will leave you with these two
kisses."

Janicah kisses Das on his lips and his forehead then lays him
gently on the sofa. Afterwards, she leaves the room then returns with
a hand-knitted blanket. While staring and smiling at her sleeping,
new friend, Janicah spreads the blanket over his body. Succeeding
her thoughtful action, she quietly climbs the steps, tiptoeing into her
room.

3
Getting Acquainted

The morning following the pouring of his soul to Janicah, Das wakes up only to see he's in the living room alone. Following a stretch and yawn combination, he stands and focuses his attention on an oil painting centered on the far wall. Slowly, he advances toward the eye-capturing portrait then stands in awe. His eyes zoom in on a little girl, sitting between a beautiful woman and a handsome young man. While appreciating the painting, Das speaks in monotone.

He Speaks

> "This young girl must be Janicah—even at a young age
> her smile reveals her passion and her love for life—
> The man who holds her must be her father—the woman
> her mother—for some reason they don't smile, I
> wonder why. From child Janicah, if this is she, her eyes
> reveal the purity of her soul; yet sadness is apparent in
> her expression—
> The two parents seem to be bitter, as if they have
> experienced something dreadful; perhaps it's my
> opinion or my perception."

As Das concentrates on the painting, Janicah enters into the house with two bags of groceries. She smiles and stands in the doorway while looking at Das stare at the painting. Softly, she closes the door, sets the bags on the kitchen floor then creeps into the living room. Approaching Das from the rear, she explains the picture.

She Answers

> "This picture which captures your eyes is all I have left
> of my family in unity—
> I damn he—that man—who held me as if he loved me,
> but he loved his mistresses, not my mother or me.
> I was two days before turning three when he decided to
> leave my mother and I to live alone—

Although I was very young, I felt the disheartening
touch of calamity—so harsh and so cold.
Like you, I've grown to know hate and the displeasures
that life has to offer; however, I needed to forgive—
I soon learned that even though I lost the most
important man in my life, God has given me the
strength to live."

Das turns toward Janicah then greets her with a welcoming hug.

He Speaks

"Beautiful is the day that allows us to again appreciate
each other's presence following a night's discussion—
Once again I've been given the opportunity to see the
elegant beauty of an intelligent and stunningly beautiful
woman."

Janicah blushes. She grabs Das by his right hand then guides him into the kitchen where she sits him at the table. Next, she puts away the groceries then begins cooking breakfast. During her duty, the kitchen remains quiet. Once the emanation of bacon fills the room, Das breaks the silence.

He Speaks

"My sweet and beautiful Janicah, your hands should not
be troubled for the means of serving a man—
They should be used for the use of your wanting;
therefore, allow that skillet to switch to my hand."

Das eases from the table then steps toward Janicah. While standing behind her, he kisses the rear of her neck, sweaty due to the heat of the stove. With one hand on her waist, he reaches for the skillet. Janicah grabs his hand then turns around. Staring wondrously into his eyes, she comments on his consideration.

She Answers

> "My desire to cook is not to serve any man, but for a
> man like you, it is my duty, my want, and my will—
> Every thought of your being here allows my shoulders
> to be free from carrying the loneliness, which I left
> on misery's hill. I want every meal prepared by my
> hands to give you the strength needed to give yourself
> mercy—
> To allow you the endurance to overcome the past
> that continues your pain and your suffering."

Das directs Janicah to the chair in which he once sat. As he
stares romantically into her eyes, he continues to speak.

He Speaks

> "A man, if he is truly a man, does not want his woman
> to give him his strength, but to remind him that he has
> it—
> Her wanting to be with him, and the thought if he falls
> she will be there to nurse him back to health are his
> concerns. I traveled to your land on a whim, unsure
> what it was I was achieving; it was strength in hope,
> which assisted me—
> Somehow—somewhere I was given additional strength
> on this mission of possible delusion and probable
> stupidity.
> Yet, believe it or not, it was your words that assured me
> I can accomplish such a task; thus I'm here as you
> wished—
> To be your servant, your king, your North Star and
> Southern Storm, and to seal our fate with a kiss."

Upon removing the food from the scalding stove, Das stoops
before Janicah. His glossy brown eyes wrestle with her glistening
hazels. After a moment of silence, the recently acquainted romancers
close their eyes, allowing each other's lips the opportunity to

meet. Following their passionate kiss, Das withdraws slowly then continues to speak.

He Speaks

> "Although my stomach hungers for this food we
> prepared together, my body desires the consent of
> yours—
> To engage in relations that should only be between two
> lovers—on the bed or if necessary, on the floor.
> I know my asking of such an activity is hasty, however,
> I've never felt this way for anyone like I do now—
> Accept my apology if I have asked too quickly, and
> please do not send me away for I need you like the rain
> need the clouds."

Surprised and excited, Janicah refrains from revealing her joy. Once a woman who told herself she'll never be intimate with anyone other than her true love, she finds herself in a predicament. Besides, she hasn't been intimate for nearly five years. Das hasn't been for several months. Looking at Das's irresistible smile, Janicah replies.

She Answers

> "Before I respond to your comment, I must tell you of
> the promise I made to myself, which is to sleep with no
> one until marriage—
> Until this moment, I've found no one worthy with
> whom I can share my mind and heart or even my soul
> or spirit.
> Suddenly, a man who seems to be the one I've long
> searched for has come into my life—
> I'm left feeling that if I were to act solely on my
> emotions, the deed we do will not feel wrong, but
> right."

Das nods at Janicah's response then asks of her mother's whereabouts. In turn, she tells him that her mother is with her friends, and her wish was for the two to get acquainted. After a smile, Das continues.

He Speaks

> "My intentions are not for a physical procurement, but
> to tie together our physical and spiritual ends—
> If I've been too forward in my speaking, then it is now
> that I beg you of your forgiveness.
> Although I have brought to you a tenet to engage in
> intimate relations, my mind reminds me of a pernicious
> past—
> Each woman who shared her body with me was left
> without a moment's notice; I was once a man with no
> class.
> My fair Janicah, I do not want to disturb a beautiful and
> joyous acquaintance by us laying in the comfort of our
> heated emotions—
> I am afraid for I fear it's possible that I have been
> cursed to make ill of any woman's heart that opens to
> me.
> As much as I want to kiss your neck, give you a bath
> and lick you places not just any man should see, it's
> best that I don't—
> For I cannot promise all will be well once the moment
> passes; thus this may result in your asking me to leave
> your home."

With a confused, awkward smile, Janicah stares admirably at Das and cuffs his face within her palms. Following a silent stare, she kisses him on his forehead. Afterwards, she stands to her feet then orders him to take a seat as she places two plates, two forks and two glasses of milk on the table. After serving breakfast, Janicah sits across from her distinguished gentleman. Das attempts to speak, yet Janicah demands his silence by bringing a finger to her lips. Das obliges, and together the two bless the meal.

Following breakfast, Das removes the dishes from the table then places them into the sink. Janicah stands beside him at the sink, both trading smiles back and forth as they wash their items. Assured that the kitchen is in its proper order, Das and Janicah continue their conversation on the living room sofa.

Ellard Thomas

He Speaks

"Surely, by now, you are aware of my immediate
feelings to have you in a manner that I've refrained
from in quite some time—
For some bizarre reason, I feel that my asking you to
be with me after knowing you by letters and one night,
I've committed a crime.
Have I allowed my lips to speak of this too soon? If so,
it's because I believe I have next to me the epitome of
all women—
Although I am hearing the drumming of my heart, my
mind still steps to the unsteady patterns of affliction's
rhythm."

She Answers

"My poor Das, you have painted a picture of colors,
shades, lines and dimensions from what you speak—
Can you not let go of a past that may hinder a fruitful
future and the happiness for which you continue to
seek?
This body, soul, and mind are one as you and I should
be; therefore, I am willing to lay with you, but be
gentle—
The time has definitely come when it is a must for you
and me to be compassionate and sensual."

Janicah grabs Das by his left hand and leads him to the stairs;
Das halts. Before Janicah can ask him what's wrong, Das lifts her
into his arms then carry her to her bedroom where he lays her gently
on the bed. Following a passionate kiss, Das exits the room only to
enter the bathroom to fill the tub with soothing hot water. Next, Das
rushes outside to retrieve a handful of orchids, missing Janicah's
call for him.

"Das where have you gone to leave me here on the bed
anticipating the feel of our bodies against each other's?
Can you not hear the yearn of my body for yours and, if
not, come here and listen to it closer!"

Upon his return into the house, Das grabs a candle from the fireplace mantle, a bottle of wine from the cabinet and a single, crystal glass. Hands full, trying not to drop anything, Das hurries to the bathroom, placing the bottle of wine and the glass next to the tub and the orchids into the water. Satisfied with the romantic ambiance, Das lights the vanilla candle then retrieves Janicah from her bedroom. As soon as the couple enters the vanilla-scented, steam-filled bathroom, Das stands behind Janicah and whispers in her ear.

He Speaks

> "Come, my love, for I have ready a soothing bath that
> will relax your body and ease your mind—
> Allow me the opportunity to relieve you from this
> attire, which covers you from head-to-toe, and from
> front to behind.
> Sit and be calm so I can wash your body and massage
> your muscles; thus your only duty is to sip this wine—
> It is moments like this that I can appreciate without
> feeling an inkling of anything that I haven't left
> behind."

While Janicah relaxes in the tub, she smiles as she watches Das lather the bath sponge. Das returns the smile as he stares romantically at his lady's flawless body. Both infatuated parties keep their silence.

After lathering the sponge, Das begins to bath his queen. Starting with her feet, he works upward and stops when he reaches Janicah's forbidden area. "Do I dare?" he asks. "As long as you're not afraid and know what to do, you may proceed. If you run into any complications, I'll assist you." Having done it before with many other women in his life, Das continues with confidence.

While carefully washing Janicah's hairless, tender area, Das softly massages her clitoris. Janicah sighs. Gently, yet firmly, Das massages his lady's breasts with his other hand, quickly becoming aroused.

Ellard Thomas

He Speaks

> "How ripe and tender can a peach be when there is no
> sign of fermentation, just the presence of purity?
> Although touching your body arouses me, it is your
> mind that I passionately lust for."

She Answers

> "To tease a woman is not only mean, it is something
> that may have her react other than lady-like—
> You have touched me in places that have not been
> touched by any other man in quite some time.
> Tell me, are you feeling remotely similar to how I feel,
> and if so, let's not wait any longer—
> As I continue to look at you, my desire to be with you
> grows hotter and uncontrollably stronger.
> I can't lie, I want to make love to you now, but first
> there's something I must do prior to our diving into
> sweet delight—
> It is my turn to bathe you as you have done for me;
> therefore, please excuse me as I rise."

Janicah hesitates to remove Das's finger from her cervical
area. Once Das withdraws his hand, Janicah sighs then steps out
of the tub. Face-to-face with her lover, she deeply kisses him while
removing his clothes. Free from the clothes he had on since the start
of his journey, Das eases down onto his knees and drops a cuffed
hand into the bathwater. As he looks at Janicah, he takes a sip of the
soapy potion from his palm.

He Speaks

> "This which I have done should reveal my feelings for
> you; if not, I know of nothing else that would reveal my
> feelings—
> From the darkness which I've walked, I dreamt of
> a light; yet, what I have here is a drop of the sun's
> healing."

One foot after the other, Das enters the tub then leans back. His eyes focus on Janicah's lathering of the sponge and her bobbing breasts. "Are you going to cover yourself with a towel?" he asks. Janicah smiles. "If you don't like looking at me, I can cover up."

"If you're comfortable as you are, I don't mind."

"Good. I'll remain naked."

After lathering the sponge, Janicah starts Das's bath, starting with his neck. Like a mother would her child, she continues to clean his ears, back, midsection, rear, legs and lastly his feet.

"All done," Janicah whispers.

"You missed a spot," Das utters while pointing to his flexed muscle.

"Oh," Janicah smiles as her eyes widen at Das's erected flesh, "let me take care of that now."

Very carefully, Janicah grabs and washes Das's hardened phallus. Afterwards, she directs him to stand and into her arms. Following a gulp of wine, Das obeys his woman's silent command.

While holding her man in her arms, Janicah dabs Das's body dry then hangs the towel on his erected flesh. The two laugh. Somewhat embarrassed by Janicah's action, Das chases her into her bedroom where they laugh and lay adjacent to each other on the bed. Once the laughter ends, anxiousness and curiosity fills their minds and bodies. Lying on her side, Janicah stares at Das who whispers an array of sweet lines.

He Speaks

> As I lay here, wandering what to do with you, I come to realize that you're simply a flawless diamond sent from heaven's cave—
> Thus far you made my journey well worth the trip; I was a merely an emotional wretch until you showed me how not to be afraid. As I lay here, parading in your eloquent and divine presence, I come to realize my risk in trusting my heart was a risk worthwhile—
> Here I am staring at a moving picture that a million words cannot describe; nonetheless, your beautiful mind and body are both simultaneously versatile."

Janicah grins. A luster of seduction fills her eyes.

She Answers

> "This day, I give to you that which is dearest to
> me aside the love for my God and my love for my
> mother—
> I beg that you take this gift presented to you, and I pray
> you cherish it more than you would any other.
> I can no longer control myself, so please allow the
> moment at hand be used for you to express how you
> feel now—
> Even if this maybe a mistake, I am sure that I can
> continue living as I have done prior to our being now."

Das turns Janicah onto her back. As he lies on top of her, he whispers in her ear, nibbling between poetic clauses.

He Speaks

> "Close your eyes and prepare your body for a gentle,
> yet, deep impact that may cause you to squirm—
> Allow my mind the freedom to touch your thoughts and
> in turn, I will become eternally yours.
> Once inside, deep or shallow, allow me to softly collide
> with the walls that surround your woman's cavity—
> Allow me the opportunity to elevate your spirit to
> another plateau, bringing you to a world that has no
> bounds or gravity."

Das kisses Janicah on her lips then grabs one of her soft, perfectly shaped feet. He, then, sucks on each toe, causing Janicah to moan. After paying special attention to each individual toe, Das massages the balm of Janicah's feet. The foreplay continues as he strokes his tongue against his lady's smooth legs. Goosebumps surfaces Janicah's skin following each touch.

With the intent to please Janicah by any means necessary, Das spreads Janicah's legs like an eagle preparing to soar and continues his oral seduction on her shaved gap. Squirming and moaning, Janicah enjoys the foreign feeling.

She Answers

> "I give you this body and pray that my doing so will not
> be a mistake, but a token of my desire to be yours—
> The gentle nibbles of your teeth, and the flutters of your
> tongue makes me feel something I've never endured."

Das continues to nibble, suck, and lick Janicah's center. As she begins to climax, he slowly enters his erected tissue inside of her. The farther he inserts himself, the tighter Janicah squeezes her legs around his waist. Noticing the agony on Janicah's face, Das cease penetration.

He Speaks

> "I do not wish to bring pain to someone as sweet and
> innocent as you, my beloved, Janicah—
> I will not continue any further because this act of
> intimacy should not be the cause of your suffering."

Janicah slowly releases the tension from around Das's back.

She Answers

> "Be patient with me for it has been so long since
> I've been with anyone in this way—
> Please continue your duty so we can finish this
> session, which will tie us forever spiritually."

Like asked, Das fully inserts himself inside of Janicah once more. The warmth of her cavity nearly causes him to climax. Quickly, he thinks about something other than the feeling of being inside her in order to stop the seepage. Unfortunately, his only thought is of his ex-girlfriend, Calia, who broke his heart a few years ago. Partially angered from the thought, the built-up pressure in Das's erection dissipates. Then in an organized fashion, he begins a series of gentle ins and outs and circular motions. Das's slow movements cause tears to fill Janicah's eyes; however, he continues to perform.

Like he has done so many times with other women, Das forces Janicah's legs by her head, penetrating deeper into her shallow cave, grunting with each thrust. Janicah bellows, but after adapting to Das's rhythm and the size of his nature, she closes her eyes and welcomes the physical and spiritual bond.

Following their episode of multiple positions and orgasms, Janicah and Das lay side-by-side trying to catch their breath. For no reason at all, the two burst with laughter.

He Speaks

> "I believe I've found the last diamond in the wroth, the
> last of hope, and my first breath of life—
> Even though the sun shines through the window and
> onto your face, it could never warm me as you have
> done."

She Answers

> "Although the sun makes a day and the moon a night,
> you have made this woman whole—
> You possess the strength of David and, yet, you
> have a gentle and divine touch that is uncommonly
> known. I ask— is it luck, prophecy, or destiny that has
> united you with a simple, yet, intelligent girl like me—
> Today, I will no longer question fate, for it is fate that
> has allowed us to blend so nicely."

Das's stroking of Janicah's silky, long black hair causes her to fall to sleep. Following a kiss to his woman's cheek, he pulls a blanket over their overworked, sweaty and naked bodies. While cuddling close to her from behind, Das whispers in Janicah's ear.

He Speaks

> "As you sleep, my enjoyment will be watching God's
> greatest and perfect creation lay calm—
> I'm left admiring the woman, who has captured this
> heart, which was once lost, but now it's found.
> When you awake, I will be here waiting for I have
> found the strength necessary to stay—

Even though we've engaged in sensual relations, my respect for you is nothing less than great."

Das snuggles close to Janicah then wraps one hand around her torso. Underneath the hand-woven blanket, they both sleep quietly.

Periodically throughout the day, Janicah and Das converse, engage in sexual acts and sleep. Soon the day turns into night and the night turns into a new day. Nevertheless, the bond between the two grows stronger.

4
The Day After

It's the come of a new morning. Das awakes to the birds' chirping. Following a lion-like yawn, he puts on one of Janicah's robes then walks to the window. He smiles as his eyes surfs the blue sky.

He Speaks

> "How can such a day of calamity and affliction exist
> when one can be grateful to see and breathe—
> To have the ability to walk and speak, and enjoy
> nature's beauty in her most precious formality."

Das turns toward his sweet, sleeping belle then looks up at the ceiling.

> "Good morning, my sweet, Lord, who gave me the
> strength to wake up next to a beautiful dame—
> Every wrong that I've endured may now be forgiven
> for my new life begins today."

Janicah slowly opens her eyes. A smile appears on her face as she watches Das prance around the room. Sore from the previous night, she eases herself into a seated position.

She Answers

> "What is it that gives you the reason to smile so
> proudly, and dance as if you're at a ball—
> That has you filled with a joy and makes you stand
> in confidence, so happy and so tall?"

He Speaks

> "It is not what, but who is it that gives me delight to
> wake up filled with gaiety and joy—
> It's not what, but who is it that gives me the reason to
> smile and the energy of a young boy!"

She Answers

> "So who is the cause of your cute, boyish smirk and
> this sense of joy you hold true—
> Who gives you the energy to prance in my robe and
> the desire to rid yourself of the old you?"

He Speaks

> "It is He, my Lord, who gives me the strength to
> prance and dance, but you are the reason why I smile—
> But it is you who allows me the ability to be free like a
> lion running through the wild."

Das jumps onto the bed then hugs Janicah. His attempt to give her a good-morning kiss is declined. Defeated, Das tries to keep cuddling to Janicah like a cub to its mother.

She Answers

> "My dear love, who wishes to snuggle to me like
> a cub to its mother, please wait—
> I also would like to indulge in your company,
> but our lack of hygiene says, not yet.
> After we bathe, we can hold each other close or go
> outside and enjoy a beautiful day—
> First, we must wash up then everything else can be
> decided on, until then, no way!"

He Speaks

> "I will not again attempt to kiss your lips, so I
> will direct my kiss elsewhere—
> Perhaps your ear that is covered by your mane, or your
> cheek; either will be okay with me.
> I know—how about the six inches above your waistline
> for it is not bias to my action—

>After taking a sniff of my own stench, I find myself
>understanding your need to withdraw without my
>asking."

After hugging her twill-smelling man, Janicah waddles from the
bedroom to the bathroom. There, she applies a facial cream to her
face then toothpaste to her toothbrush. While brushing her teeth,
Das joins her at the sink. Before he has the chance to say anything,
Janicah quickly places her index finger to her man's lips.

She Answers

>"For one moment, I want to look at you without your
>words of influence and seduction—
>To stare wondrously at your flawless, yet, sculpted body
>with great admiration and appreciation.
>Although physical appearance is of temporary delight,
>your body is truly a sight to see—
>It is this silence right now that allows me the
>opportunity to further see you as an outstanding being."

Das removes Janicah's finger from his lips then brushes his
teeth. While doing so, he stares graciously at his lover's body. After
rinsing his mouth out with peppermint mouthwash, he speaks.

He Speaks

>"How does a woman still look beautiful even after
>the actions of a previous night's wrestle—
>To still be as eye-capturing as a rose standing strong
>and alone in a garden of weeds.
>Looking at you makes me wish I would've come
>to your doorstep a lot sooner—
>For two people to only know each other for a short
>time, we are definitely for one another."

She Answers

>"If you can recall, it was words similar to what you
>speak, which started our sexual duo—
>I suggest you put a stop to your compliments before

we are forced to put on another show!"

Das stands in front of the mirror and stares at his reflection. Janicah stands behind him, wraps her arms around his waist and looks over his shoulder. As the two look at the happy couple, Das ruins the moment.

He Speaks

> "It is surreal that I have found a woman who may be
> possibly a reflection of me—
> And, if like me, her outside beauty may hold secret
> her true feelings of how she is to be.
> Should I whole-heartedly trust her even though I've
> never truly trusted anyone before?
> I'm torn between then and now; however, I find myself
> doubting the mercy and kindness of the Lord."

Astonished and confused by Das's choice of words, Janicah interjects.

She Answers

> "I do not fully know what exactly it is that you ask of
> me, but I must tell you I'm honest with everyone—
> From my initial response to your letter to my first sight
> of you, I've been nothing less than truthful!
> Please, do not retract the sweetness you've shown me
> for it is your sweetness which draws me to you—
> Within your speech, you said I am possibly the
> woman's reflection of you, but I say not true!
> In front of me stands a man who chooses to wrestle
> with a past, which he can no longer do anything
> about—
> Behind him is a very strong woman who is willing to
> help him see a bright future; however, that means taking
> a different route. Don't doubt me for I have given
> you no reason to nor said anything remotely close to
> profane—

In order for you to join me in the gardens of bliss, it's
going to take your will to change!"

Janicah plants a kiss on Das's back. She notices three, long,
thin marks parallel to each other, running diagonally from his right
shoulder to his lower left torso. With two fingers, she gently traces
the middle mark. Das sighs then without Janicah's asking him to
explain, he chooses to do so.

He Speaks

"Those marks you see are to remind me of the abuse I
received when protecting my sister from Cheetah—
Although I was strapped then whipped like a slave,
it gave me pleasure to know at that moment Amecca
didn't suffer. As you can see, misery will be tattooed on
me until the day God calls me to his kingdom—
Each day that pass, I pray for the chance to see him
again so I can inflict upon him the same pains he had
given me."

Janicah shakes her head with sadness. Following another kiss
to Das's back, she runs a bath. Das says nothing as he continues
to stare at his reflection. Tears fill his eyes as thoughts of his past
occupy his mind. After taking a deep breath, he watches as Janicah
enters the tub and, within a matter of minutes, he squats beside her.

He Speaks

"Am I a man who does not know redemption or
happiness when it appears before my face?
Sadly, I'm nothing more than a vase of havoc's roses
and affliction's tulips; yet I'm kept alive by disgrace.
I've had the opportunity to taste bliss when I first
entered through the doors of a great woman's home—
Thank you again, Janicah, for it is you who have
allowed me to see a side of myself never before
shown."

Das kisses his well-relaxed Janicah on her cheek. His sudden
touch awakens her and causes her to suddenly splash bathwater

onto him and the floor near the tub. Following a cute, girlish smile, Janicah responds.

She Answers

> "What is it that brings you here to squat by the tub
> like a puppy waiting for its owner?
> I am sorry for wetting you; perhaps, I will be forgiven
> once I allow you to come in here."

Das attempts to enter the tub, but Janicah tells him to stand still. Her eyes widen at the size of his dangling phallus. With a smile on her face, she grabs Das's nature. However, Das becomes filled with agitation.

He Speaks

> "What is it about this part of my body that puts
> such a look of happiness on your face—
> That makes you act like a child receiving its biggest
> gift on a long awaited Christmas day?"

She Answers

> "I only question how something that size can bring
> me pain and pleasure simultaneously—
> That when inside of me, it touches every spot making
> me cry tears of happiness and glee."

Das slowly removes Janicah's hand from his erected flesh.

He Speaks

> "Forgive me, Janicah, for I do not wish to engage in
> physical intimacy, but to sit and relax with you—
> To have this tension removed from my body, and enjoy
> this moment of extreme value."

Janicah looks at Das with astonishment. Her smile quickly hides behind a frown as Das sits himself between her legs. Partially disgusted, she nudges him forward then exits the tub in a hastily fashion.

She Answers

> "I have ended the soaking and the bathing of my body;
> therefore, I will ready myself for today—
> I did not mean to add anguish to your anxiety, so
> I will leave you here to finish your duty!"

He Speaks

> "Why do you suddenly exit the tub in a hastily
> fashion and leave me alone?
> Could it be because of my not wanting to be intimate,
> or is it because of the action I've shown?"

Janicah holds her peace then leaves the bathroom with a smirk. As soon as she enters her bedroom, she lies on her bed then begins pleasing herself, whispering.

> "A woman knows her own pleasure and exoticness; for
> what reason do she need a man?
> All that a man can provide her besides mental anguish
> is a warm penis, and yet, we still improvise.
> Here I lay naked with the want to be intimate with my
> man, but he has declined my offer—
> It is this reason to why I lay here touching myself, and
> it's this reason to why I will not bother him."

Once Das finishes his bath, he strolls into Janicah's bedroom. Upon entering, his eyes widen to Janicah's self-pleasing performances. As he watches her fondle her breasts and massage her clitoris, he becomes aroused. Quickly, he rushes to her aid with the intent to fulfill the request he had declined in the bathroom. Unfortunately, as he attempts to get on top of her, Janicah pushes him away with her foot. Unaware of defeat, Das removes Janicah's finger away from her clitoral area and tries to insert his erection. Again, he's pushed away. Hoping to get some type of positive reaction, he removes Janicah's finger and replaces it with his tongue.

His action is accepted. Yet, while she enjoys Das's oral seduction, Janicah smiles and applauds her own thoughts.

> "A woman's power can win wars and reign victoriously
> over any man's ego—
> A woman knows exactly what she wants and how to get
> it; in my opinion, a woman's mind should be deemed
> illegal.
> I wait to exhale as my man's tongue flutters back and
> forth in the same fashion as a dolphin's tail—
> Wetness comes to my cervix from the consecutive
> touches of my man, which are so light and so soft."

Once Janicah reaches orgasm, she taps Das on his shoulder. "Thanks," she whispers. After receiving the signal that his duty is complete, Das tries to insert his hardened muscle once again. Surprisingly, Janicah turns onto her side. Confused and filled with tainted feelings, Das heightens his determination of making love to Janicah only to be forced to give up. Frustrated and mildly hostile, he turns onto his back, muttering his feelings.

He Speaks

> "How shrewd is the woman who involves herself in an
> intimate act only to gain her own satisfaction?
> Here I lay with my nature in my palm while my woman
> lies on her side undistracted.
> What have I done to deserve such treatment for only
> wanting the feeling she and I shared before?
> I see that I'm not a patron of her heart, but an employee
> working deliberately for her own amusement."

Still on her side and turned away from Das, Janicah rolls her eyes then reply to her man's whining.

She Answers

> "Hear these words I say to you because they will be the
> answer to your questions of implications and disrupt
> feelings—

It was not me who decided that I was not interested in
the touching of our bodies; I believe it was you.
In the bathroom, I wanted to be pleased, yet, instead, I
received an unexpected decline to my offer—
I was bothered, thus my reason for coming in here to
please myself; unfortunately, I had to be my own lover."

Sadly this issue begins Das's and Janicah's first quarrel. Both
parties rant and rave about whose feelings are more important. Upset
and not wanting to argue any further, Janicah attempts to leave the
bed. Beyond her surprise, Das yanks her arm, forcing her to the
spot she once occupied. Astonished by Das's inappropriate action,
Janicah swings her arms and kicks her feet at her attacker. After
being slapped once and kicked twice, Das overpowers Janicah and
pins her arms over her head. Janicah screams and struggles to get
free. However, all of a sudden, she hushes and relaxes after seeing
the burning anger in Das's eyes. A flashback of being molested by
her uncle forces her to turn her head away. "Do what you must," she
cries.

Looking at the tears running down Janicah's face, Das
immediately releases Janicah's arms then removes himself from
over her. Sorrow fills him as he thinks about what he had just done.
Without saying as much as one word, he flees from the house,
running naked through the streets like a mad man, ignoring the
pointing and gossiping spectators. Quickly, Das finds refuge in the
park, trying his hardest to conceal his nudity between the bushes.

While Das hides in the park behind a bunch of bushes, Janicah
lies on her bed crying. A film of disgust covers her trembling, naked
body. Head in her pillow, she sobs.

"Castration should be brought to any man who dare
uses his penis as a weapon and his strength as a
prison—
May he who cannot saddle his own actions be lifted
away from women then thrown into the devil's pit.
As I sit in this room of anguish and ill temperaments, I
am haunted by the horrific memories of a young girl—

Oh crucial world that has hexed me with discomfort
and malice, I salute you with rebuke!"

To lessen her anger and frustration, Janicah cries and rips apart her pillows. In the meanwhile, two officers find Das walking bare-ass through the park. Cautiously, the two policemen approach the nude beau while telling him to stand still. The larger and darker of the two advances toward the nude fellow, then ask him the reason for his public nudity. With tears in his eyes, Das whimpers.

"Why must articles of clothing cover my carcass when I
am already concealed by disgust?
Physically I am sculpted like an angel, yet, the
foundation of my soul remains and waits to be crushed.
I've wrongfully touched someone who I care for more
than any riches or my great achievements—
Although the sun shines on my skin, I am chilled by the
actions that I've done to my beautiful woman."

Once subdued and forced into restraints, Das is forced into the rear of the police wagon. Upon arrival to the jailhouse, he is then escorted inside and given a raggedy, oversized, black outfit to wear. Afterwards, the two arresting officers rush him to a room that has one table and one chair. While sitting in disbelief, he cries, "I'm suppressed by agony while misery seduces me. No more will I ever hurt another. No more will I cause anyone else to suffer."

After being alone for four hours in desolation, the head chief enters the room. "Stand up," he orders. "I have some questions to ask you." Das slowly rises to his feet. Once the head chief removes Das's restraints, he asks the perpetrator the reason for his indecency. Das ignores the officer's question then rambles.

"I am not an occupant of your beautiful city, but a
mere traveler visiting his destiny—
I should not be put behind bars for my actions;
however, I should be in the arms of my lady.
Save me from this imprisonment for I have
acknowledged my indecency was a disappointing
action—

My word is all I have to offer you; therefore, I beg you
take the gamble of releasing me."

Leaving the prisoner in the room in arm braces and shackles, the
head chief and the two arresting officers meet in another room to
decide Das's fate. There, they laugh at the foreigner and make jokes
about him.

As Das sits, awaiting the verdict, Janicah becomes worried.
Alone, with no one to talk to, she advances down the stairs and
mopes into the living room. From the couch, she stares through
the window, watching the transition of the day turning into dusk.
Worried, she paces back and forth for approximately thirty minutes.
Afterwards, she returns to her room, kneels next to her bed then
speaks to the Lord.

"Hear my voice, my good Lord, for my eyes cry and
my heart beats nervously in a rapid cadence—
Where is the man you've delivered to me like an angel
from the heavens? Where is he?
Today I've learned that in the heat of aggression there
are no winners just losers—
Please forgive me for the amount of negative energy
that surrounds my unclothed flesh."

While Janicah lies on her bed thinking about Das, he thinks
about her too. All that he had done to her also occupies his mind.
After being alone for nearly an hour, the officers return. But before
the head chief has the opportunity to say anything, Das utters.

"I've done great deeds of fallacy to myself and the
woman who I hold dear—
The reason to why I am here is due to an action I
thought I had left in my past years.
It is here that I must stay until I am with no aggression
for I refuse to hurt anyone I care about—
I shall sleep on your concrete bed, eat your foul food
and watch the rats walk proudly with smiles."

Surprised, the officers look at each other with doubt. The head chief then asks Das from where he is visiting. Once the head chief receives Das's story, he comments.

"You're indeed stranger than any other man I've arrested and those I've sentenced to execution. Why is it you speak with a liquid tongue and a heavy heart?"

Das looks directly into the head chief's biddy, brown eyes. Following a smirk, he answers.

> "I was once a jagged edge until I was smoothened
> by the words of a perfect woman who I recently
> abandoned—
> She sits upset in a house and possibly crying because,
> before her eyes, I went from a man to a phantom.
> I give you permission to shackle my arms and my feet
> so I cannot harm anyone else who cares for me—
> Send me to the starved dominions that await a lost and
> damaged spirit so they can devour my soul savagely.
> It will take merely a few hours before my thoughts
> of happiness rot; therefore, this time tomorrow I'll be
> ready for death—
> I shall not bargain for my life, however, I pray that you
> pay visit to my Janicah and let her know I grievously
> wept."

Following a mute silence, the head chief tells Das that he is free and, if he is to stay, it will be under his own duress. Das pleads his guiltiness and assures the officer he needs to be locked away. The head chief shakes his head, sighs deeply then looks to his fellow officers for their opinion. Neither says anything. Fresh out of answers and suggestions, the head chief fulfills Das's request by ordering his subordinates to escort the prisoner to a cell. In a matter of moments, the head chief and his fellow officers bring Das to a dreary, single man cell. Once inside, Das asks the head chief for a sheet of paper and a pencil. "For what reason do you need these items?" the head chief asks. "It so I can write a letter to my Janicah," Das replies.

"Fine. Officer Sleir, please bring this strange fellow the items he wish to have."

"Will do, sir!"

Officer Sleir retrieves a sheet of paper and a pencil then gives them to Das. After thanking the officer, Das scribbles a message to Janicah. Once complete, he asks the head chief if he could kindly have someone deliver his note. "Why should I do such a thing, Treymone?" the head chief grunts. "I shall speak no more if you do me this favor," Das utters. After receiving Janicah's address, the head chief assures Das that someone will visit Janicah tomorrow. Relieved from worry, Das takes a seat on the cold, concrete bench, and then wails.

In the meantime, as Das undergoes his mental breakdown, Janicah lies alone on her bed. Her pillows are torn apart and soaked from crying. Following hours of being frustrated and worried, she falls asleep to the gentle melodies of the wind hitting her bedroom window. Twice she is awakened by what she believe are knocks. Unfortunately, it is the branches periodically hitting the window.

5
Hell Day 4 Janicah

During the dawn of the next morning, two officers knock on Janicah's door. Awakened from a deep sleep, Janicah jumps up with excitement, hoping the knocks are from Das. Quickly she ties her robe, slide on her slippers then runs full speed down the stairs. After opening the door, a look of deceit replaces her smile. Two officers stand before her— Officer Jilo Meynant, a tall, dark gentleman with a thin mustache and Officer Danma Fierre, a light-skinned, cleanly shaved fellow. After greeting Janicah, Officer Meynant apologizes for the early disturbance then hands her an envelope. Awed by Janicah's beauty, Officer Fierre breaks from his silence. "Yes, like my partner said, we apologize for this intrusion. It was by the request of a bizarre man named Das Treymone that we come by and deliver this letter. Don't worry yourself, he's safe, but he is a prisoner under his own will."

"What happened?" Janicah questions.

"He was found naked in the park," Fierre cackles.

"I see. Well, I know where to find you two if I need you any further."

Janicah closes the door then hurries to the sofa. Partially comfortable, she rips open the envelope then reads the letter carefully.

He Speaks

> "My dear, sweet Janicah, who I love more than the
> woman who brought me yelling into this world—
> I cannot face you for I've done something horrific to
> my beautiful and precious pearl.
> I am now in a place that will allow me to be free from
> anger-driven motives and actions—
> Here is where I belong—behind bars scarred by my
> own acts of distaste and dissatisfaction.
> I've concluded that I am no better than any other man
> whom you've previously loved and cared for—
> Please understand that I love you more than the air that
> keeps me breathing and the life I no longer care for…"

Janicah pauses momentarily from reading. Her eyes fill with tears. The weight of silence sits on her shoulders and weighs her further down into the sofa. As tears fall onto the paper, she continues to read.

> "I am a thief who flees prosecution through the
> possibility of doubt and technicalities—
> I've stolen the hearts of women who dared loved me
> and once again, the verdict is guilty.
> I cannot escape this cloud, which hovers over me nor
> this path paved with good intentions—
> Sadly, I missed my opportunity for a blissful life even
> though it was less than inches away!"

Janicah presses the letter against her chest and whimpers like a puppy in a storm. Without warning, her mother enters through the front door only to see her daughter weeping. As quickly as she can, Janicah's mother hurries to her saddened daughter. "What's wrong, Nicah?" she asks then sits next to her daughter. Janicah rests her head in her mother's bosom then tells her all that had happened. Janicah's mother suspires then continues to console her daughter. After a few minutes of being held, Janicah excuses herself then rushes up the stairs. Her mother, on the other hand, continues sitting for a couple moments, grabs a few items from her room then leaves again.

In the interim of preparing a bath and gathering her clothes, Janicah stubs her right, pinky toe against the leg of her bed. While screaming in agonizing pain on the floor, she starts her menstrual cycle. Toe throbbing, eyes swollen from crying, and blood trickling down her thigh, Janicah cries out.

> "Damn it! Damn it! Damn it! Lord, why must I now
> be approached with hinders!
> I sit here on the floor with a possible broken toe, but
> worse of all, I am beginning to cramp!
> I'm feeling damp between my legs and feverish in
> my head, oh why now Lord?
> Today it seems you have allowed Mother Nature
> to come at an awkward time without any warning."

After spending moments on the floor, Janicah finally accomplishes the fret of getting to her feet. Afterwards, she hobbles to the bathroom where she takes a squat on the toilet. Although faced with obstacles, her determination to get to the prison to see Das takes precedence.

> "Although I suffer the pains of a woman, my intent to
> to leave this house will prevail—
> Today is a day when anyone who decides to stress
> me will be a contestant of hell's wrath."

Janicah cleans herself up then limps in pain to the tub. Each agonizing step brings her closer and closer to relaxation. Nearly slipping into the tub, she regains balance then carefully enters the hot, bubble-filled tub. With no time to truly relax, she washes up quickly. Afterwards, she gallops from the bathroom to the bedroom embraced by pain, anger and confusion. With little hesitation, she pulls a cry-baby-blue dress from the closet then quickly grabs her undergarments. After rubbing lotion on her gentle brown complexion, she begins getting dressed. While putting on her dress, thunder-like knocking comes from the front door. Unaware of her mother's absence, Janicah ignores the knocking. Again, the thumps interrupt her.

"Mother, will you please get the door?"

Janicah waits for a response, but only receives three more knocks.

After concluding her mother isn't home, Janicah rushes to the bathroom to ensure her satisfaction with her attire. Frustrated and flustered, she grabs her purse then hobbles cautiously down the stairs. Once she reaches the door, astonishment joins her nervous look after opening it. Officer Danma Fierre stands before her with a smirk.

> "Forgive me if I'm disturbing you, but my intention
> is to check on your safety—
> I understand lately that you have been stressed by
> possibly more than Das Treymone.
> I know I was here before, but he insisted that I come to
> tell his sweet tulip to cry no more—

71

> And to see to it that you are with a smile for his
> absence is entirely on his own."

Although Danma's second visit was without Das's consent, but of his own desire to see Janicah, he smiles. In turn, Janicah replies.

> "I sincerely thank you for your willingness
> to serve and protect, but believe me, I'm fine—
> It just so happen I am on my way to the cellar
> to go see that bull-headed man of mine."

Danma tells Janicah that he's willing to accompany her to the jailhouse. Sensing the flirtatious intent in his voice, she welcomes his company. Within an hour they arrive at the stone-built building, which imprisons Das. Like a couple, the two walk up a small set of stairs then enter a room where Janicah is asked to sit and wait until arrangements are made.

After leaving Janicah alone for thirty minutes, Officer Fierre returns. "It is time," he announces. Janicah rises to her feet and accompanies the officer to Das's cell. While standing in front of Das's cell, Janicah stares at her man lying face-to-wall and singing joyfully on the bench. Suddenly, Das turns toward the familiar vanilla sent. His eyes widen. Happy and flabbergasted, he asks Danma to leave him and Janicah. "As you wish, you crazed fool!" Danma barks. As soon as the bars open, Janicah rushes into the cell and hugs Das. Appreciative of her action, Das slowly withdraws himself then asks Janicah to sit next to him.

He Speaks

> "I came to realize I am a particle, which is sometimes
> never seen and many times brushed away—
> I have a name, my only identity—Das—three letters
> that are still unusual to peoples' ears.
> I cannot posses fear for it's a hyphen
> -separation of my soul from my body
> -separation of my spirit from my God
> Yet, I've been created as 'normal' – two feet,
> two hands, two eyes and only one sight—darkness

Like other men, I have five senses—touch, sight, taste,
hear and smell, all heightened to recognize this plague
of anger—
It wears me like a cloak and allows me to be choked by
the thoughts of self-destructed danger."

Janicah takes a moment to digest Das's unseasoned words.
Afterwards, she answers.

She Answers

"Forgive me if you are unhappy to see me, but
as a strong woman I am also your backbone—
If you should fall in the deepest of holes in the
earth, it's my duty to bring you back home.
The moment you forced yourself on me, I was
reminded of an action in my past—
I wasn't entirely upset with you, but at the action
which seemed uncontrollable in your grasp."

With his dirty hands, Das grabs Janicah's left hand and kisses
it. While looking into her eyes, tears drop from his own. Quickly he
turns away.

He Speaks

"Those that you call nightmares and those
that make you scream, I call dreams—
Those whom scatter about like rodents to leave
friends and family to suffer, I call teams.
I hear the written words that are painted as
pictures within life's frame—
Ignorance has stained my garments while love
has delivered to me torture and pain.
I feel the rain when the sun is most dominant during
the early day and late morn—
I'm in search of a needle sharp enough to start the
mending of a heart which hate has been torn.
I've been born into a world where sensitivity is
flooded by ignorance and selfishness—

Ellard Thomas

> Although I've survived the battle alone, I am
> in this war trembling, cold with helplessness.
> Your blue sky is my black, muddy ground that I
> will continue to walk on after my death—
> Although I inhale and exhale, life will not exist to me
> until I'm with my last breath!"

As tears fill her eyes, Janicah kisses Das on his dirt-smudged cheek.

She Answers

> "I say our mistakes are teachers and motivators that
> exist to better us throughout life—
> You have done nothing wrong for I take full
> responsibility for not being by your side.
> If I had a wish, it will be that you come home
> with me to sit in front of the fireplace—
> I honestly say that this place isn't for a man who is
> capable of creating beauty from hate!"

He Speaks

> "I live in a room with four walls and a ceiling—chaos,
> revenge, stupidity and ignorance, all roofed by
> malignity—
> Although I have a birthday, I do not exist; nevertheless,
> my entering this world was a mistake
> If you were to fish at my lake, you would feel the
> vicious pull and bite of the hunted—
> Swiveling on the hook of life until the presence of death
> darkens my sight and expels my breath.
> My death will not be remembered or recorded for
> my eyes open only to close—
> I am the weed that is unnoticed and unwanted that will
> forever struggle to be a rose.
> If I shall die, do not fill a box with my body, instead
> fill the air with my ashes—
> May those who cared not to know me, suffocate, as

if they been fed fragments of glasses.
Take me as I was born Lord, unclothed and
screaming for your divine mercy—
I know what services life provides; however, I want to
be a child playing happily in your nursery."

She Answers

"Das, the day is growing old, preparing to give birth to
a new morning tomorrow—
You are a free man who chooses to be imprisoned
with so much guilt and much more sorrow!
Come with me so we may go home and sit together
and make plans for our future—
As long as you have me in your life, I promise
to be your truest friend!"

Das slowly rises to his feet then leads Janicah to the cell's bars, yelling for her release. Like a flash of light, Officer Fierre appears and orders the opening of the bars. As he reaches for Janicah's arm, she pulls away then stares at Das and continues.

"The line between asinine and stubbornness is thinner
than the line between love and hate—
If you add them both, it equates to an erroneous formula
whose solution is a devaluated fate!"

He Speaks

"Go and abandon me for I ask you to be
merry without this hindrance—
Always remember that my heart belongs to you and
this body belongs to this prison!"

She Answers

"You speak like the weak that blames defeat
on the accord and actions of others—
The tongue of a man is sharp enough to pierce
a woman's heart; does it not pierce his own pride?

What else would it take to show you the potential
of two souls in peace and harmony?
I have wept many tears over hours, and why
is it that I still cry?
I say you are a fool, Monsieur Treymone, who role-
plays a character that don't exist—
I will leave you with this last hug, this last tear,
my last ounce of love and this last kiss!"

Janicah cuffs Das's face and gives him a quick peck. Tears
running down her cheek, she quickly backs away and exits the cell.
Escorted by Danma Fierre, she looks back and waves farewell. As
Janicah becomes the outline of an image down the hall, Das looks at
the only person he ever cared about leave his circle of dismay. Once
Janicah's outline becomes nothing more than a memory, Das turns
his back to the bars and stares at the brick wall with its markings of
previous tenants.

"The palace of the shepherd is in the fields amongst
the sheep to act as scarecrows to the wolves—
Standing erect and firm to the galloping of claws
and discrete snarling of rage and animosity.
Never cower to the eminent approach of defeat,
where there lies confidence lies triumph—
Even casualties of war never die in spirit, although
their corpses vegetates the earth.
I rise to the clapping of an unnoticed audience
entertained by mediocrity—
I play advocate to the destruction of this world
by the hands of dominion's!
I reside in a residence of indecisiveness where no one
can differentiate truth from opinions—
My strategy is a tragedy, which brings chaos to those
who bare witness to my immorality.
To bring sight to those stricken with cataract so
they can perceive my achievements—
I have grown immune to the virus called hate and
numb to the bacteria labeled vulnerable.

When I speak, it will thunder, and where I cry, it will
flood valleys and melt tundra—
When the sky chooses not to become gray, my eyes will
mist with precipitation and ready to pour!"

6
The Unannounced Visitor

Four days has passed since there was any contact between Janicah and Das. Each day Das sits in his cell speaking to himself, eating only once a day while Janicah is visited daily by Officer Fierre every evening around four o'clock. That which started off as routine visits by the officer matured into an uncontrollable obsession. Amazed by the officer's persistence in courting her, Janicah continues to decline the officer's offer of dating; nevertheless, she enjoys his company for it helps keeps her mind off of Das.

Late afternoon, on the fifth day while Janicah sits and jokes with Officer Fierre, Das makes the decision to return to Janicah's home. Fortunately, he realizes that he was a fool for not leaving with his benevolent queen. Following lunch, he demands his release.

"Gentlemen!" Das hollers. "Let me out!"

Officer Jenone rushes to Das's cell. With a questioned look on his face, he releases Das from the iron and concrete cage. Smiling and still wearing his filthy, mangled clothes, Das hugs the officer.

"I beg that you do not do that again, Treymone." Officer Jenone warns while leaning away from the foul smelling, former prisoner.

"My apologies! Ah—today, I feel as if I cannot be saddened by anything. I'm going to go home and worship the ground on which my lady walks."

"I see. Well, an officer went today to check on her well-being."

"Good."

While keeping his distance, Officer Jenone escorts Das to the duty desk. There, the officer of the day looks at the filthy, smiling Das then shakes his head, keeping his silence as he completes the Prisoner Release forms. Following his signature on the forms, Das traipses toward the exit. Before leaving, Officer Jenone stops him.

"Treymone!"

"Yes, Officer."

"I'm sure your journey is far, I will take you home. I wouldn't want you to do anything foolish."

"How nice. Thank you."

Officer Jenone accompanies Das to a police wagon, both taking their respective seats. As they journey on the path towards Janicah's home, neither the officer nor Das says anything. Although holding his silence, like a field mouse tiptoeing on cotton, Das's smile grows larger each moment the coach advances closer and closer to his queen's home. Finding Das's expression particularly comical, Officer Jenone chuckles at his profane thoughts of his passenger.

Once the police coach arrives to Janicah's house, Das quickly jumps off. After thanking the officer, who frowns at the sight that another police coach is present so late in the afternoon, Das skips to Janicah's front door. Respectfully, he waits until Officer Jenone becomes a particle down the road.

During Das's waiting for Officer Jenone's leave, Janicah continues to laugh and talk and drink tonic with Officer Fierre, unaware of Das's decision to come home. While laughing, Janicah bends forward, accidentally spilling her drink onto the officer's uniform. After apologizing for her clumsiness, Janicah leaves to retrieve a towel from the closet. Thinking it's the perfect moment, Danma removes his uniform pants. When Janicah reenters the living room, she drops the towel at the sight of the half-dressed officer.

"Danma," Janicah smiles, "please put on your pants."

"There's no reason to play this game any further, Janicah. I want you, and I'm sure you want me."

As Danma advances toward Janicah, knocks on the door stops him in his path. Suddenly, Das enters and becomes immediately irate at the scene. Without hesitation or question, he rushes in, pushes Janicah from his strike zone then throws a punch to Danma's face. After knocking the officer down, Das begins a sequence of sporadic blows to the officer's stomach and head. Appalled by Das's actions and his blatant disrespect for her home, Janicah pulls the emotional warrior away from his enemy. Blood seeps from the officer's nose and mouth as he staggers drunkenly to his feet.

"Believe me when I say you've just signed your own death certificate, Treymone! You insane bastard."

Held tightly by Janicah, Das remains silent as he watches Officer Fierre exit with his pants in his hand. Shortly after the officer's parting, Das snatches his arm away from Janicah's grasp.

Ellard Thomas

He Speaks

> "These past five days was the closest to hell I
> could've been until now—
> Yes, my body is matted with dirt, but I am
> still cleaner than this house!
> It is trickery of my woman that allows me to
> speak profanely with a bladed tongue—
> I look at your beautiful face and see that even
> a pure light allows darkness to come.
> I will leave so you may play in the hurt emotions
> of a man with no known satisfaction—
> The taste of imprisonment is more divine than this
> aroma of deception and retraction!"

Janicah walks toward Das until she is merely inches from his face. Looking up to his five-foot-nine frame from her five-foot-three stance, she unleashes her own feelings.

She Answers

> "From your distrust with all those who have hurt you,
> blindness has come to your sights—
> Although you have eyes and they open like blinds in
> the day, you will forever see nights!
> Have I done wrong or have I been wronged by the
> man who says he is for me?
> I paid visit to a man whose decision was to stay
> hidden from his self and further more, me!
> I didn't wish for the situation that brought such pain
> to your already misconceptions—
> If one should be filled with fury, it should not be you,
> but me; yet I'm crossed like intersections!
> I came and you said leave, I spoke and you said speak
> not and here I am under your judgment—
> I will live like those who are of innocent decree and
> will plead not guilty to your assumptions!
> So you say you will walk, I say run and find yourself
> amongst the ruins of dismay and foulness—

I will be the mother to my own heart and exclude
anyone who dares act childish!"

Like a gust of strong wind, Das blows by Janicah, nearly
knocking her off balance as he heads toward the front door. Instead
of exiting, he slams the door shut and returns to where he stood.
Weighed down by his pain, he kneels on his left knee and asks
Janicah her feelings for Danma.

He Speaks

"Is this man—this officer, the one to replace me and
if so, were you going to let me know?
My head is bowed low for I am saddened by what I
saw; Janicah through my veins, anger has joined my
blood flow.
Behold, it is a man on his knees begging for your
answer
and will not move until I receive your word—
Although my thinking is possibly absurd, it is my wish
to hear you say I am no longer needed to be yours!"

While holding her breath against Das's foul stench, Janicah rubs
her man's nappy hair and answers.

She Answers

"I can say much, but little will work best for now;
especially since you are drowning in a sea of adrenalin
and ill feelings—
I have no feelings for Danma; to say the least, his action
was something I didn't want for I love this bizarre man
kneeling before me."

Janicah helps Das to his feet then escorts him to the bathroom,
assuring him that her love is only for him. Once in the bathroom, Das
runs a bath as Janicah readies his clothes. In a matter of minutes, she
limps back into the bathroom only to see Das sunk in the water, his
eyes shut. At her entrance, Das speaks.

Ellard Thomas

He Speaks

"I wish you could feel the ridged edges of a heart,
eroded and crenellated by the waves of torment—
Awaiting the moment to be healed and deployed from
its state of dormancy!
If you look through this man's eyes, you will see a child
with disfigured perceptions of how to love—
Crawling from attachment only learning to walk the
path of seclusion and exemption.
See him grow weary due to the abandonment of light
and strong to your care—
Yet he's unable to bare the intensity of his own thoughts
and for anyone who dares enter be aware.
This man who you see as ambitious, inspiring and
independent needs you more than breath that gives him
life—
Each word and hug that we share is a step closer to you,
bringing me further and further from my demise.
Take me as a white rose bud to a place I can fully
bloom in the garden of your warm smile—
Each moment and every second away from you is
excruciating like walking without shoes over a hell's
mile!"

Janicah sits on the side of the bathtub in pain, trying to not let
Das notice her agony. To Janicah's sigh, Das opens his eyes and sees
the painful frown on Janicah's face.

He Speaks

"Whatever complications that brings you agony
and misery, I beseech you to tell me—
What is it that puts a painful expression on such a
smooth, beautiful face?"

She Answers

"I have pains in my abdomen from the visit
of a woman's monthly flow—

I have an aching in my pinky toe so immense
that it causes me to hobble.
You never noticed because your focus was on
yourself and not on me—
I mean no distaste towards you, but please understand
that cramps have come upon me!"

When finished with his bath, Das exits the tub cautiously. Janicah slowly rises to her feet then gives him a towel, helping him dry his restless body. After tying the towel around his waist, Das follows Janicah into the bedroom where he holds her tight and kisses her passionately. Noticing the tiredness in her man's eyes, Janicah orders her worn-out man to lie down and rest. Upon his getting underneath the sheets, she kisses him on the head and informs him of her needing to go to the market. Das smiles and, after laying down for a couple of minutes, he falls into a deep sleep. Janicah smiles then leaves the room quietly, hurrying as fast as she can to the marketplace.

While Das sleeps, a nightmare of his death causes him to toss and turn. Suddenly a loud boom followed by men chanting "Treymone!" startles him. Partially terrified, Das leaps from the bed, jumps into his trousers then flees from the room. Before he has the opportunity to challenge the excitement, Officer Fierre meets him at the top of the staircase. "Don't be surprised, Treymone. I told you that I would return, didn't I?" Baffled, Das throws his hands in the air then gets ambushed by seven uniformed men. While stepping backward, in order to give himself room from the angry mob, he stumbles and falls against the wall, hitting his head. As if planned, Officer Fierre and one of his colleagues grabs Das by his feet then drag him down the stairs. Das tries to kick himself free; the officers' grasps tighten. "Get your paws off of me you bastards!" Das yells. The men laugh and continue to drag the helpless man down each of the stairs responsible for Das's headache.

While Das lies at the base of the stairs, suffering from a headache, Officer Fierre stands over him. "If I recall correctly, you bloodied my nose and swollen my cheek. I shall now do you the same favor!" Officer Fierre pulls back his right fist but is quickly stopped by the head chief. After the head chief pushes Fierre aside, he asks Das if he had hit the officer. Das nods, yet, before he is given a chance to explain, the head chief gives his men the signal to commence beating. As he tries to find a way to get to his feet, Das is hit consecutively with blows to his head and stomach. In need of a wider area, the men drag the battered young man to the living room where clubs replace their fists. Although beaten, Das's fighting spirit doesn't allow him to stop the attempts to his feet. Each time an opportunity presents itself, he gets slammed to the floor. Blood continues to flow from his mouth like lava from a volcano as he is kicked over and over in the midsection. Suddenly, the barbaric mob stops the beating then laughs at the bloody, bruised victim.

"Look at him, he's had enough," says one of the officers.

"I agree," another officer utters.

"No, I want him to suffer," Fierre controls. "Any man who hits me deserves to die..."

During the brief recess, Das struggles to his feet. To his surprise, four officers throw him against the living room wall, securing his arms to his side. With a smirk, Officer Fierre advances toward the beaten beau. "Monsieur Treymone doesn't look so tough now, does he?" Without warning, Das spits a wad of bloody phlegm and mucus in Fierre's face. "That wasn't smart," Fierre threatens. After wiping the disgusting sludge from his nose and lips, Fierre knees Das in the crotch. "Now that you're bent over, kiss my shoes!" Fierre taunts. Hunched over in pain and agony for a few moments, Das's legs fail to keep him standing. Like an apple falling from the tree, Das drops to the floor. Just before the men recommence the beating, the head chief calls them all to attention as Janicah enters the house. Shocked, baffled and angered, Janicah drops the market bags to the ground and rushes over to Das, pushing each officer out of her path. Once to him, she squats down, grabs Das's head and curses the intruders.

> "You bastards who say they serve and protect
> will forever be my foes—
> You've come into my house with disrespect and
> neglecting the peace that this home has come to know!
> Why did you come here and bully one man when
> there are many more of you—
> You claim to be men, I say you are cowards and pray
> that God bring war upon you!"

The head chief approaches Janicah slowly, standing a foot away.

"Madame, I am the head chief, Captain Leuvre. I am aware that this is your home, but this man has done an unlawful deed."

"What is it that he is guilty of?" Janicah asks.

"Treymone admitted to hitting Officer Fierre. Therefore, this is his punishment."

"What? He only did what he did because he was protecting me from Danma's sexual advances!"

The room grows quiet. Suddenly whispering amongst the officers cracks the silence. Every eye sets on Officer Fierre who smirks, yet says nothing.

"Fierre," the head chief grunts, "is this true?"

"It was her fault, Captain!"

"Fierre, your badge then an apology to this man, now!"

Fierre frowns at his superior as he gives him his badge. Afterwards, he smiles at Das then returns his focus to his captain.

"Sir, I will do no such thing!"

"Very well, we'll discuss this at the station!"

The head chief apologizes for his men's actions then explains that the station will pay for all medical expenses and damages done to the house. As the officers gather at the door, Das struggles to his feet with Janicah's assistance then speaks to the crowd.

"You will feel the raft of a man who has nothing to lose
except the life you tried to take—
You will feel the draft of a wind so strong that will tip
over each of you involved in this disgrace!
Hate is not a word fit to describe the emotions filling
my heart or the blood warmth rushing through my
veins—
Your fatal flaw was to allow me to keep breathing;
therefore, there will surely be a life that I'll claim.
Yes, I received a beating like one that is given to slaves
only for being a man for my lady—
With the strength I gain to heal these bruises, I assure
you that one of you will not see another day.

You say you're sorry, but I say put to sleep your
meaningless, tired and lame apologies—
Little to your knowledge, you have awakened a giant,
which will trample your confidence and bury you in
your shame!"

The head chief orders his men to leave the premises. Afterwards,
he glares at Das.

"Treymone," he utters, "as captain of the Santa Lucia Police
Station, I must warn you that a war due to this justifiable mistake
would be catastrophic for you!"

"If so, then it shall!"

Hand on his side and blood running down his face, Das points
to the door. "Leave, now!" At his command, the head chief exits.
Suddenly, Das collapses.

He Speaks

"Janicah, I have brought shame to your home when all
I wanted was for you to be happy—
I've soiled your home of peace with my presence;
therefore, I understand if you decide to be mad at me!
I've been beaten badly to the point that I cannot see
neither your face nor your smile, clearly—
My arms, back, legs and face may be bruised; however,
it is a must I take my revenge—hate stands near me!"

She Answers

"I should have never left you alone after that heated
battle between you and Officer Fierre—
I will get you a towel for your face so don't go
anywhere and just lay right here!"

Janicah leaves the living room, picks up the goods dropped from
the commotion then enters the kitchen. Shortly after, she hurries up
the stairs. "Warm or hot towel, Das?" she yells from the bathroom.
She waits for a response, yet one isn't received. "Warm or hot,"
she repeats. After not receiving a response the second time, Janicah

rushes down the stairs only to see a trail of blood leading to the open, front door. Sadly, she whispers to God.

> "Oh good Lord who gives me life, I ask you
> where has this man of mine gone?
> It is late and no stars light the nights; yet he
> walks these dark concealed streets!
> Oh Lord, protect him and bring him where
> he belongs, which is here at home—
> I pray for I know you will do as you have
> done before and bring him to me!"

As Janicah cleans up the mess made by the abusive gang, Das walks the streets without shoes and a shirt. Evil intentions overcome his thoughts as each step brings him closer to indefinable rage.

While walking near Nique tavern, Das catches sight of Fierre entering and laughing with his friends. Fortunately for Das, he remains unnoticed like a shadow wearing a black cape. Almost overwhelmed with happiness, he searches his area for something that could be used as a weapon. To his left—nothing but rocks; to his right, the same. Coincidently, a broken bottle lies before him. Holding his side, he bends down and picks it up. Next, in a very calm fashion, he walks into the tavern and sees Fierre and his two friends sitting, laughing and drinking at a table in the far back. With Fierre's back faced to him, Das limps through the crowd's stares and quiet whispers until he is within a foot of Fierre. Catching sight of Das, one of the two friends grabs Danma's attention by pointing to the bloody image behind him. With a quick, two-hundred and eighty-degree turn, Fierre's eyes widen with surprise. Before he has the chance to stand to his feet, Das lunges the jagged bottle into the side of Fierre's neck, allowing him to flutter like a fish without water on the floor. Everyone stares at Das who smiles at his dying foe. "You have spoken many words, yet you will not say anything— anymore!" Following his comment, Das slowly turns around, tempting the two friends to challenge him; smartly, they don't dare. Instead they scurry away like frightened mice.

Still filled with rage, Das looks at his near-decease enemy then kisses his forehead. "Although you were my enemy in life," he whispers, "we may be friends in death!" Worriless, Das rises to his feet then exits Nique. Suddenly the tavern bursts with screams and loud talk.

While limping down the streets in triumph, Das rambles.

> "I love the thought of dying for it reminds me this
> world is close to ending—
> I love the way I'm pictured as a genuine individual,
> but I am a broken heart in need of mending.
> I love how the thought of this world pleads innocent
> to times past to these current events—
> The executions of the innocent, the freedom of the evil
> and the wrongs of elected officials.
> I love the image I'm given from friends and family;
> however, it's not close to how I see myself—
> I'm fatigue from worrying, restless from thinking and
> exhausted from dealing with everyone else's mischief."

Swaying side-to-side as if drunk, Das staggers down the rue, clenching his ribs. Fatigued from fighting and being beat, he finally reaches Janicah's house following a two-hour journey. Upon stumbling through the door, Janicah notices the fresh blood on her man's hands and pants. Refusing to question his whereabouts, she looks down at the floor then gives him a fond embrace. Afterwards, she helps him up the stairs and into the bathroom where she runs a bath and helps him out of his clothes. During her bathing of her bruised companion, Janicah doesn't say a word; neither does Das.

After completing his bath, Das hobbles behind Janicah into the bedroom. Both hurt parties lay closely to each other on the bed. Held by the woman he loves so much, Das closes his eyes and allows the tears to race down his face. Coughing and trembling from pain, he whimpers.

He Speaks

> "Forgive me for I may have brought war upon
> a home that knows only peace—
> I walked the streets tonight with rage until I found
> Officer Fierre with his friends, laughing and drinking.
> Forgive me for all the ails I bestowed upon a soul that

only wanted happiness and love—
Like a rug, it's been taken from underneath you;
however, I promise it will be again as it was.
Although I have sight with one eye, I can still see the
most valuable of all the world's diamonds and gems—
You are a fully blossomed rose that I refuse to be
unprotected; therefore, I continue to be the thorns on
your stem!"

Janicah holds Das tighter than before. She becomes subdued to an odd feeling of him leaving her.

She Answers

"Rodents scurry, cowards flee and patrons follow, but
you lead with your feelings and your mind—
To me, you will forever be a man whether death
takes you or the winds of time!
You are so kind when you're not angry, but I understand
the reasons for your purpose tonight—
Sleep now my king for it's time that you rest with
your loving queen by your side!"

Janicah gently slides her hand over Das's face, forcing him to close his eye. Within a few minutes, he falls asleep. Very softly, Janicah rolls him onto his back, rises from the bed, and then, hobbles quietly to the window. Her eyes fill with tears as she wishes to change the outcome of the day. Suddenly hit with cramping in her midsection, Janicah returns to the bed then lies in the fetal position.

Shortly after Janicah falls asleep, Das wakes up in the mood to be intimate and attempts to remove Janicah's nightgown. His unsteadiness awakes Janicah who informs him that she is at the end of her menstrual cycle. Das acknowledges her concern but doesn't care for his only desire is to make love. Following a deep sigh, Janicah gives consent. Happy that his woman has chosen to let him have her, Das places a towel underneath her backside. Carefully and with great consideration, Das's intimate session ends after fifteen minutes. After he wipes his lower region with his bath towel, Janicah excuses herself and goes into the bathroom to wash up. Once she returns, she cuddles with her beaten man. Calmly the two fall asleep in peace.

7
Notice to Leave

Once again, awakened by knocking, Das puts on a different pair of trousers. Without waking up Janicah, he proceeds down the stairs and opens the door. Chati stands before him.

"May I help you?" Das asks.

"Let me guess, you're the man from Dalay. How are you? I'm Denmon Chati, Santa Lucia's most trusted delivery man and good friend of young Janicah and Claire Mi'Voir. Are either of the ladies home?"

"Janicah is upstairs sleeping, but Madame Mi'Voir has chosen to stay with a friend for my duration in Santa Lucia. I assure you that I can sign or take anything for either of them if you'd like."

Chati tries to refrain from staring at Das's face, but curiosity defeats him.

"May I ask what happened to your face?"

"I rather not talk about my bruises, Monsieur Chati. Now, if your business here is done, I suggest you come by later."

"Wait—wait—wait a minute. You're Das Treymone, right?"

"Yes."

"The letter I have here is for you."

Das accepts the letter then wishes Chati a good day. Afterwards, he closes the door then takes the letter to the sofa, wrestling with the idea of who could have sent him the letter. He recalls only telling Kristoffe of his whereabouts. After opening the envelope, he reads the letter inside.

> *My oldest son who I have grown so far apart*
> *from, I need you now—*
> *I am stricken with an illness and with this stiffness in*
> *my arms, I need you around!*
> *Your brother told me you are with a woman you*
> *went to see on a whim—*
> *I told you that God will grant your wish if you*
> *only pray and ask Him.*
> *I apologize if this is an inconvenience for I know*
> *you deserve the best ever—*

91

Before I leave this world, I need my offspring
to come to me like inclement weather!
I know I have not been the best friend due to
my decisions and my mistakes—
I wish you could understand that I didn't mean
to choose a man to be my escape!
Let the past journey on its own and the future
make its own path—
I miss your smile, your sarcastic jokes, your hugs
and most all your goofy laugh.
Just the thought of your being away from me makes me
want to close my eyes and cry—
The thoughts about my not being there for you
makes me want to close my eyes and die.
I survived the strong currents of havoc's rivers and the
chills of misery's winters—
Though my heart beats for now, it won't be
whole until you return its center.
I can say sorry forever, and I know it won't be
enough for your sadness and grief—
The first friend I had was you; therefore, I hope
you know it is the truth which I speak.
Many times your words strengthened my weak
soul and now that I'm strong, I can go on—
Better late then never right? I'm just upset
that I lived my life so short—so wrong.
My marvelous son, who I have not seen for
years, please come to me—
I am dying from internal bleeding, stemming from
what a man from my past have done to me.
I still smile because I know you will receive
these words before I am deceased—
Just the thought of you possibly coming home
allows my strength to increase.
Be merry, my child, for I will await your arrival
and then pass over to God's kingdom—
See you soon my son for right now I will
allow the time you need to quickly come!"

Das drops to his knees. Tears flow like rivers from his swollen eyes. He regrets not seeing his mother for so long. As he cries over the letter, Janicah steps quietly down the stairs in her robe, following the snivels. From behind, she puts a hand on Das's shoulder.

> "Tell me love, what is it that makes your eyes
> stream like that of rivers—
> That is making you breathe heavy and which makes
> your body shake and shiver?"

Das motions to his feet. He stares with sorrow into Janicah's eyes and says nothing. Janicah waits for him to say something, yet he doesn't. Without warning Das mopes into the kitchen, leaving Janicah standing confused in the living room. Soon she follows Das, joining him at the kitchen table.

He Speaks

> "My stay here has only been two weeks and
> I already feel compelled to leave—
> During my stay, such dramatics has happened, like
> my hurting you and the beating I received.
> Last night I left here to seek out he who is named
> Fierre, but who I rather call coward—
> This letter is the climax of this drama, and surprisingly
> enough, it was sent here by my dying mother.
> Indecisiveness has crossed my path of sweet bitterness;
> yet I am unsure of what to do—
> Although my heart says to stay here with you, my
> mind says I must return home, soon!"

Janicah rises from the table then sits on Das's lap. She replies as her right arm comforts her man's neck.

She Answers

> "I have met a great man—a man who posses a
> heart greater than a king—
> Yes your stay here was quite of interest but
> it brought to me no suffering.

Ellard Thomas

I say go see your mother who is ill so her
rest will indeed be in peace—
Even though I will be sad, it is your duty to ensure
your mother's relief.
It is fate that has brought us as one, so it
will be fate that will unite us again—
After last night's murder, it is my suggestion
that you leave here this instance!"

He Speaks

"Desolation has no acquittal so I say it
will be fate that will judge me—
Although I'm being held by my woman, the
arms of catastrophe are those that hug me.
I cannot leave you alone and let your heart
carry this burden; therefore, I'll stay—
If I am verged upon by vengeful men, I will
carry out the verdict of whatever it is they say!"

She Answer

"If you were to leave it will dishearten me, but
your death would be unbearable—
When you are away with your mother, just know
my pain will be tolerable.
If you don't leave as I've asked, I fear the coming
of a vast destruction—
Destruction to my soul and my heart, and the
start of more affliction!"

He Speaks

"My decision is made my lady, so to further
this conversation is redundant—
To be away from you is a tragedy in itself
that I cannot handle in its abundance!
The circumference of my circle is complete
as long as you're the radius—
You are the link that connects my heart and mind;
this is why I am so reluctant!"

Das nudges Janicah then rises from the table, crumbling the letter in his hand. After shoving it into his pocket, Janicah looks at him with fury and grabs his wrist.

She Answers

"Take heed to my advice and go to the woman
responsible for bringing you into this world—
Would you rather live with regret and grief,
or are you willing to sacrifice your temporary hurt?
If you won't leave on your own accord then
I say you must leave this house now—
Please Das, go to the woman who should matter most
and don't feel that I'm kicking you out!"

He Speaks

"Why is it you yell at me as if I cannot
hear if you speak in monotone?
I do understand that my absence is warranted
and it's your desire to be left alone.
If I have over welcomed my stay, please forgive
me for my unwanted intrusion—
Since this is your home and not mine, it is
my pleasure to leave you in seclusion!"

She Answers

"Try to understand that I have run out of
pleasant words to make you leave—
In your heart you should believe the one who
needs you most is nearly deceased.
Why shall we disguise the inevitable when
certainty is in it's truest form—
If you don't decide to leave, it will be I who'll
cast the stone to make you go!"

95

Ellard Thomas

He Speaks

> "The betrayal in your words has stricken me,
> leaving my heart in carnage—
> In one moment a strong man has been weakened
> and left with his feelings garnished!
> Suppose I trot back home where my mother
> lay motionless and perhaps breathless—
> Here I stand before you—a man to serve you, but
> for some reason I feel reckless.
> While you ready breakfast, I will ponder the thought
> to vacate your divine premises—
> My face is scarred, yet it is my heart that
> carries the darkened blemishes!"

She Answer

> "Underneath that pillar of woe, you know what
> I say is what needs to be done—
> If you love me as you say, then this task
> at hand needs to have no reasons!
> We can argue or bargain, but the journey awaits
> your decision to go ahead and proceed—
> Don't let fear or the thought of losing me hinder
> you for I say, there's no need!"

Nearly at his breaking point, Das brings his battered face mere inches of Janicah's.

He Speaks

> "Don't let the fear of losing you not hinder
> or alter my decision, you say—
> It was my decision to come to you that put
> me in this situation in the first place!
> Why do your eyes tear at the thought I may
> abandon you as you've asked?
> Why do you say leave when you want me
> here with you as long as my life lasts?
> Let your flight of care for my mother crash

96

and burn to the ground—
I will go, my sweet, Janicah, for love has shown
its face and turned back around!"

She Answers

"You speak of wickedness like those who've
been beaten savagely—
Your sweet core has been eaten by your own
gnawing of weakness, oh what a dire tragedy!"

Das interrupts Janicah before she can finish her debate.

He Speaks

"You've dared to say I am weak, but I say it takes
more courage for me to stay—
To live in salvation with you and face the punishment
that may soon come my way!
You have looked into my eyes and seen what
makes this man so headstrong—
For me to leave this palace of subtlety would
be considered a choice so dead wrong!"

She Answers

"Wrong you shall be, but dead you shall not
if you would listen to me and go home—
If it makes any difference to you, I am very
willing to pack my things and come along!
Before you speak, please allow me to finish what
I need to say in the next sentences—
The man I have grown to know is showing me
much of his stubbornness and incompetence!"

Das turns from Janicah and darts up the stairs, stumbling over
the first step. Regaining his balance, he completes his climb then
flashes into the bedroom. After grabbing his suitcase, he throws his
clothes inside, ranting and yelling profanely. As quickly as possible,
Janicah hobbles up the stairs and enters the room after him. To her

surprise, Das shows no acknowledgement of her presence. To the sound of Janicah's sighs, Das glares in her direction and continues his path of rage.

He Speaks

> "This triage of assaulted words has allowed time to
> go by like early autumn drafts—
> I will no longer parade in the perplexity of cries
> from a woman who is so filled with craft!
> At last your wish for my absence shall be granted
> and I pray to God you stay merry and well—
> It is by the ridicule of my own emotions that seems to
> keep me emotionally delicate and frail!"

She Answers

> "Stubbornness runs idiotic through your mental
> and your state of delusion—
> Somewhere behind that thick skull lies intellect;
> perhaps, under your mounds of confusion!
> For some reason, you're choosing to be dim-witted for
> what purpose, I cannot fathom—
> The syringe that is inside of your mouth has prickled
> me deeper than anything else that has happened!"

He Speaks

> "Abolish your sensibility to these issues
> that requires many tears and tissues—
> I have not left, nevertheless, here I stand wooing like
> I already miss you!
> I want to kiss you, but I will not, due
> to my own sorrow, agony and grief—
> The tree undergoes many changes in the autumn;
> thus I am now the newly fallen leaf!"

She Answers

> "You do not fall due to the autumn season, but
> to the gravity of your own emotions—
> The stir of echoes in your ears are those that
> come from your spiritual commotions!
> Hush up and listen to the hollow sound that
> comes deep from within your heart—
> It is the thumping of an innocent man who is filled with
> jagged edges and ends so sharp!"

He Speaks

> "A woman knows nothing about the challenges
> that a man must go through—
> Trying to satisfy women when he does wrong
> from each follicle to his every molecule!
> Look at the embroidery of the marks on my
> face and the bruises on my back—
> It's for being a good man protecting his woman
> only to be savagely attacked!
> React act not with your words of 'go' and 'come'
> for a man can do no right—
> Trust me, my young, Janicah, the flight of misery
> has landed so I'll leave before tonight!"

Frustrated and perturbed, Janicah leaves the bedroom, slamming the door behind her. Tears in his eyes, Das continues packing without breaking concentration. Once finished, he bursts through the door and hustles down the steps, nearly knocking over Janicah who maneuvers from his path of anger. As soon as he reaches the front door, Janicah confronts him.

She Answers

> "Do not leave in haste without saying goodbye
> or without giving me a hug and a kiss—
> I beg you to not leave in this state of mind,
> which causes you to treat me as a mistress.
> This is my last plea whether you leave with rage

or whether you leave in harmony—
Do not let my last sight of you ruin the image I have
of a man who is so caring and warming!"

He Speaks

"I can no longer be tempted by your words of
joy or your speech of splendor—
In the center of this man lays a heart that knows
no springs or summers, just winters!
Get your hands off me so I may leave you
dazzling here in your generosity—
It is by my own will if I decide to go off filled
with injured emotions and animosity!
Possibly, I may come back or I may stay afar to keep
you abreast with serenity—
Eventually, this time we'd spent together will be
forgotten and so will its futility!"

Das removes Janicah's hand from his back and throws it to her
side. Following a sorrowful stare, he darts out the door, refusing to
let Janicah see him cry. Quickly he escapes the hurtful area. Janicah
runs after him, yet, stops short of catching him.

She Answers

"Tomorrow knows nothing about today, but I know
I love you and will forever—
I am strong although your speech has abraded me like
a whipping belt made from pure leather!
Before I met you, I was the silence of an empty soul
that tried flying without feathers—
Through countless endeavors I tried to show you
that there's hope even in affliction's deserts!
Instead, you developed a belief structure based on fear
and a system you've given a name to—
You were a wanderer in search of a fulfilling destiny
and I say that is what you came to!

Now, I see it has rained through the roofs of your
temple of devotion and your home of commitment—
I can see clearly through the fog of your anguish, baring
witness to your fight with resentment!
Contentment is what you are in search for, but the path
you follow leads to nowhere—
I would accompany you to the end of this circular rock;
this path you walk is one we both cannot share!
I ask that you promise me before you come back here to
look within yourself for remission—
Only then you will be able to live life to its fullest
extent without the worry of misty visions!"

After listening to Janicah's comments, Das lowers his head then
quickens his pace toward the train station. Sadden by her man's
actions, Janicah returns in to the house and leans against the door.
Silently she prays for Das's return and stands impatiently waiting.
After a few moments of not hearing knocks, she opens the door only
to see the front yard. Sadly, Das is nowhere to be seen. Overcome
with hurt, Janicah closes the door and slides to the floor, tears stream
down her face. Along with her emotional anguish, the pains in her
abdomen challenge her. Unsure of what to do, Janicah pounds the
floor with her fist, cursing men in the process.

"We are more than creatures who bear offspring and
slave graciously in kitchens—
Listening to them bitch about they're horrible days
and all their sexual tensions!
We are the suspension, which carries their egotistical
vehicles that travel low and high—
A man knows nothing about life until he's able to find
all he wants in a wife!"

Following her ranting, Janicah finds strength in her legs to run
up to the bathroom. In the meanwhile, Das walks to the train station
upset, held by sorrow.

"Why is it that I run from situations I cannot control
or those I can't find appeasing?

I've pushed away those who love me only to keep close
all of whom are considered indecent.
I cannot figure out why it is I cannot live the
way a man should live—
I curse the dealer for dealing me a hand
that requires a poker face to win!
It's obvious I am ready to fold because what I hold
are no flushes or even a set of twins—
My tears bring the taste of melancholy from my eyes to
the two corners of my lips!
The taste is salty, similar to the way I left Janicah, but
it is a must that I move along—
I cannot believe I am calling it quits on a woman
who showed me nothing but love!
She kissed by bruised face and tended to my abrasions;
was there to listen, yet never judged—
Perhaps my truest destiny isn't happiness; perhaps it's
to live unhappily without love.
Oh dear God, please watch over Janicah and protect her
from anything and anyone foul—
The reason that I continue to live is probably my choice
to cry in pain, sincerely your wretched child!"

After walking an hour and a half, Das arrives to the train station. Much to his surprise, the train to Dalay isn't scheduled to come for another twenty minutes. Quietly, he sits on a bench next to a waiting passenger, retrieves a pad and pencil from his suitcase pocket and then writes Janicah.

He Speaks

"I forgot to thank you for the hospitality you
have provided a stranger—
If you were to divide salvation and calamity by
by sorrow, I would be the remainder.
I am not writing regarding the feelings I need
to handle with myself—
But a letter of appreciation to you—a person who knew
I needed to go find myself.

A woman of your statute does not need to quarrel
with the sorrow I gave you—
I wish somehow there was a way I could send a
kiss and have it relayed to you.
I ask that you don't hate me, but pray that I will
return as a king for his queen—
I find it hard to believe that I actually had the
opportunity to find the woman of my dreams!
Now, it seems the thunder is louder than the rain;
however, my love will forever pour for you—
I want to be able to sit and talk with you, bathe you,
and open doors for you!
I want to be able to rekindle a fire that seems to have
burn low due to no pyre—
I want to be the final piece for your heart and give
you all that your soul desires!
Remember this if you don't remember anything else,
I truly love you dearly—
I am about to board the train and go as you've asked;
I look forward to the time you'll be again near me!"

To the train's screeching from within the distance, Das folds the letter and writes Janicah's name on it. At the call of "All aboard" he stands and hears a disturbing call. "Monsieur! Monsieur!" cries a little beggar boy to a dark, heavy-set fellow. "Is there anything I can do for you to earn some money? My momma and poppa are sick and my sister and brother are without food." The heavy-set fellow pushes the young boy to the ground then waits in line to board the train. Das shakes his head then approaches the fallen young man, helping him to his feet. "Young man," he says. "I see you would like to earn some money."

"Yes, I am. It's…"

"Worry not for I will give you what you need only if you do me a favor!"

"Yes."

"Take this letter to this address. Do you know where this is?"

"I can find it."

"Let me tell you…"

103

Das hands the boy directions to Janicah's home and enough money to feed his entire family. Afterwards, the little beggar sprints off into the distance. Once he disappears, Das boards the train. Although Das tries to refrain from crying, tears escape through the slits of his eyes. Tear after tear rolls from his swollen eyes, down to his cheeks. His journey back home begins as the train sets in motion.

While Das sits miserably on the train, Janicah sits on the sofa, holding a shirt he had forgotten to pack. Jolted by knocks on the door, Janicah wipes away her tears with her sleeve then leaps from the couch. Smiling at the thought the knocks are from Das, she quickly hurries to the door. When she opens it, reality strikes her with the club of disappointment. Before her stands the young boy Das sent, wearing pants with holes and a dingy coat.

"Madame," he greets, "I'm here to deliver this from a man who gave me money to do so!"

"This man," Janicah replies, "where is he?"

"On a train!"

"Good boy. Give me the note then hurry home, okay?"

"Yes Madame!"

After receiving the letter, Janicah unfolds it then mopes toward the sofa. There, she flops down and read Das's message. Following the reading of the note, she sinks deeper into the sofa cushions and weeps.

She Answers

"I darn the wind that blows agony to a village
whose foundation is built on affection—
Here I lay trembling from the bitter cold of
loneliness, walking an unchanged direction!
Perfection is the path I've learned to achieve, yet my
destiny tells me it is failure—
Dressed in the garments of disapproval, hand-tailored
by demons who all work for Lucifer!
Whosoever says the answer to a question lies within
the lips of the one who asks it, I say not—
I ask how could a heart that knows love for another turn
blind to a life that may rot!"

Janicah cries herself to sleep. When she awakes, her eyes open to complete darkness. After turning on a lamp, she ensures the security of her home then retires to her bedroom where she continues to sob.

8
The Arrival

Guessing that his brother is scheduled to return to Dalay, Kristoffe waits patiently at the train station. Bizarrely, he is correct. He smiles as Das steps from the train.

"The prodigal son has returned," Kristoffe jokes.

"Yes he has," Das utters.

"I didn't expect you back so soon!"

"Let's just say my absence was greatly needed! If you didn't expect me, how did you know to be here?"

"We're brothers. My being here was solely based on probability. Your coming here after receiving mother's letter then…"

"Enough, Kristoffe."

As the two brothers walk to their coach, Kristoffe stares at Das's face; yet he refrains from commenting. After they mount the coach, Das feels his brother's urge to comment on his face.

> "My brother who I haven't seen in weeks, I know
> you seek an answer to your question—
> I was involved in a fierce fight with an idiot who
> caused me so much infliction!
> I fought one-on-one with an officer who made passes
> at my sweet Janicah—
> Later he rushed me with a crew of his angry men
> who beat me with fists and Billy clubs!
> My brother, I killed the man responsible for my
> unnecessary beating and his friends' horrific deeds—
> After a few heated words with Janicah, and the letter
> from Mother, I left with God's speed!"

Kristoffe ponders the information for a moment. Following a deep sigh, he reasons with his older brother.

"Perhaps we should revisit Janicah then kill the others who were involved in this crime. See, I told you to say home."

"That you did, Kristoffe! That you did."

During their journey, Kristoffe informs Das that De Ano, Amecca, and Missilia are at the hospital with their mother. Das remains silent. When asked if he would like to go home to drop off his luggage, he simply nods his head then refrains from speaking any further. For the duration of the trip, neither brother says anything else.

Once the two brothers arrive home, Das leaps from the coach then shuffles to his front door. Tears roll down his face as he enters. Looking around, he sees that everything is in the same manner in which he left it. "Brother," Kristoffe utters, "I'll put away your things while you freshen up." Emotionally hurt, Das obliges with silence. Quickly, he runs to the bathroom and readies a bath. Filled halfway, Das enters the soothing, hot water. Thoughts of Janicah run wildly through his mind. Eyes closed, he whispers.

> "Arrogance is my description, and I am
> now labeled as a murderer—
> I was told time is the best healer, but it is time
> that told me to look no further!
> I remember as a child, a man doesn't cry
> nor does he show sentiment—
> Am I to be questioned whether or not I am a man,
> the answer is nonsense!"

Das finishes his bath, puts on his garments, and leaves with Kristoffe. For awhile, neither brother says anything. Yet, within a mile of the hospital, Kristoffe breaks the mold of silence.

"Das, I know you still have issues with mother, but I beg you say nothing of a profane nature."

"Kristoffe, I will speak whatever comes to my lips. Now, if you don't mind, I would like to be quiet."

"Okay!'

When they arrive at the hospital, Kristoffe leads Das to their mother's room where the other siblings surround the dying woman. At the sight of their brother's face, Missilia, De Ano and Amecca place their hands over their face in excitement and in awe. Their mother weeps with glory. Slowly, and still sore from the brutal fight, Das enters into the room of eminent death. Once he reaches his mother's bed, he hunches over then gives his mother a fond embrace. Tears of joy fill his mother's eyes as she gently brushes the back of her hand across her son's bruised face. Without hesitation, Das grabs his mother's hand and kisses it. Afterwards, he asks the others to leave the room.

"Why must we leave?" Kristoffe asks.

"Kristoffe, must you challenge everything I say?" Das growls. "I need to speak to mother, alone!"

Sensing the hostility in their brother's voice, the siblings leave. Once they close the door, Das speaks to his mother.

He Speaks

> "Here you lay close to death; yet, you are willing to
> give me your last words—
> You and I haven't shared conversation in quite some
> time; it's mainly due to my hurt!
> Curds of dryness fill my throat because I am
> at a lost for things to say—
> I came as you asked, not to see you die, but to
> get answers to questions of yesterday.
> Mother, I have played and swayed in the falls of
> obtrusions you didn't dare warn me about—
> We were the best of friends, yet due to a man your
> choices quickly turned me about.
> I dare not shout even though the hurt from memories
> past still fester like blisters—
> As you know, I was only fifteen when you asked me to
> take care of my younger brothers and sisters!
> Forgive me if I am sharp with words, but I lived
> incapacitated with revenge and rage—
> Never once I've blamed you for asking me to take care
> of the family; however I do today!"

Das grabs a chair and brings it close to his mother's bed and continues.

> "My poor, dear mother who suffers with regret and
> questions of whys and how comes—
> I do hold dearest those you taught me; for instance,

how to lie, how to fight and how to run.
I didn't come here to sadden you, but understand
sadness was my father and my mother—
It was my cover when I looked for refuge and it fed my
hunger for loneliness and my resentment for others!"

Das's mother ponders all that her son says. Not wanting her son to see her cry, the well-aged, ill woman turns her head. With a strenuous attempt to sit up, she looks at her son's face and replies.

She Answers

"I was once strong when you were merely a child and
would fight to death if needed—
Until that one day I fought with Cheetah, I
somewhat felt lost and defeated!
Sometimes a woman will take a side of a man just
because she thinks she ought too—
My beatings and the molestation of your sister I know
still comes to haunt you.
I was shown that love hurts, and it was normal to
be beaten and do whatever a man says—
As an older woman, I know now that you can't believe
solely in the words that a man says!"
Das, I was wrong, and I now realize there's no
correction to this test we've already taken—
Each night I pray you keep the strength that as a
parent I could not possess!
Allow me to provide you a list of my torments of gifts
of those I been with—
Stitches resulting from a stab by Cheetah and an array
of confusion from Monsieur Ramitz.
Only two men I've endured relationships with, which
was enough to hate all men—
The losses were more severe than any pain could come
upon me; losing all my kids!
I know suffering as much if not more than you; the
difference is that you were blessed with the strength—

The length of time that has come between us still
doesn't allow me to blow away this stench!"

He Speaks

"I remember there once was a time when your
tears use to fill me with remorse—
The source of my burdens came to me when my mother
and friend took a different course!
I forced myself to like anyone you'd considered
a partner or a significant other—
I have taken shape of a broken circle in search of
peace so I would no longer suffer.
I am moiré with infliction of a devastated past that
the sun alone cannot dry—
I've already been spiritually killed; therefore, this is the
reason why I cannot emotionally die!"

Amecca interrupts the conversation between Das and his mother
by slowly opening the door. Noticing they are deep in conversation,
she returns to the hall with the others. Following Amecca's
considerate leave, Das's mother responds.

She Answers

"It was the 23rd of September when I gave birth to
a ten-pound, eleven-ounce baby—
Tears came to my eyes for I knew he would grow to
become the man he deserved to be!
It was at that moment I knew I have been blessed with
everything a young girl could ever have—
That we would grow together as friends, having cries
and most importantly of all, sharing laughs.
You see, Das, the puzzle of life cannot be put together
until all of your pieces are collected—
Sometimes they come to you, other times they are
hidden; nevertheless, they combine to become a
message.

For a long time I became skeptic to anything that would
familiar or resemble happiness—
Through the blackness I've encountered, my light was
the thought of my oldest child, Das!"

After speaking to his mother for thirty minutes, Das is again
interrupted by his brothers' and sisters' entering the room. When they
surround their mother's bed, Das grows upset due to the intrusion,
stands to his feet and then exits the room hastily. Following a couple
of moments, Amecca catches up with him before he reaches the
men's restroom. "Das!" she hollers. Das turns around. Amecca
hurries to him.

He Speaks

"If you followed me to discuss matters that happened
in mother's room, you're wasting your time—
Although I am happy to see each and every one of you,
anguish in regards to our past still fills my mind!"

She Answers

"I overheard the words you have spoken to mother, and
Das you were truly wrong—
Here she is in the hospital, close to expelling her last
breath, while you sing a crying man's song.
I know mother isn't perfect, and things in life we
encountered were horrific, yet we live—
Is it not possible for you to learn to be friendly again,
and can you learn to forgive?
You act as if you cannot do any wrong, or that you can
walk with an omnipotent presence—
I say this to you, my dear brother, she is the reason to
why you and I currently exist!
At this moment, I'm happier than I could ever be
because you are here with us and not away—
It is okay that you stay filled with sorrow, but I beg
that you suppress it until after today!"

He Speaks

111

"My sister who I care about more than any woman
aside the others in our family—
Let's change the subject at hand, and why don't you tell
me how you and your husband are doing.
Do you remember when I told you that I never learned
to love or trust anyone ever again?
I traveled afar to meet this special woman who shared a
lot of the same things that I did.
I finally was able to rid myself of these sheets of
loneliness that have now become blankets—
I am weighed down by these anklets of fury while
moving inches away from all positive changes!"

Just as Amecca begins to reply, a skin-trembling scream comes
from their mother's room. Suddenly, a team of medical individuals
in white suits rush down the hall then bursts into the room. Das and
Amecca look at each other then quickly follow.

"Hurry up, Amecca!"

"I'm with you, Das."

Upon entering the room, the brother and sister see a doctor
and three nurses hunched over their mother, covering her like rain
clouds over a city. Kristoffe, De Ano, and Missilia stand against the
wall crying. Slowly, Das advances towards his mother's bed only to
have his arm grabbed by a nurse.

"Sir, I need you to stand back," the nurse orders.

"That—that's my mother," Das responds. "Is she going to be
okay?"

"We have the best medical team checking on that right now. So
please, stand next to the others."

Das does what the nurse orders and comforts his siblings.
Minutes after the children's watching of the medical team's display
of a rescue mission, the doctor slowly lifts his head. Staring at Das,
he shakes his head apologetically. Filled with fury, Das removes his
arm from around Missilia, bursting profanity while beating on the
wall. As he curses and swings violently, the nurse leaves the room
and returns with two security guards who subdue the out-of-control
young man. Held down against his own will, Das becomes even
more irate to the cries of his two sisters. Struggling to break free,

Das is eased to the floor, pinned helplessly. "Let him go!" Amecca demands. "He doesn't deserve to be treated like this!" Tired from struggling, Das lies on the floor. Tension no longer inhabits his body.

Once the security guards feel that Das is capable of controlling his violent nature, the two brutes lift him to his feet, preparing for another outburst. Trying to regain control of his wobbling legs, Das glances sorrowfully at Amecca and the other siblings then approaches the bed. Eyes locked on his mother's motionless body, he gently pushes aside the doctor and the nurses. Unfortunately, regret and grief from what he said to his mother during his one-on-one conversation covers his soul like a black cloak. In a room filled with cries and sniveling, he holds his mother's lifeless body tight and whispers.

> "You were my strength and my sun for darkened days;
> each time I endured pain you made me smile—
> It is because of me why you possess these beautiful
> grays; for my aid you would walk barefoot over
> desert miles! Many trials you adjourned, many tears
> crept from your eyes and many disputes solved by
> compromises and kisses—
> Many times I should have told you the truth, but I lied;
> now truthfully, I admit you are the best of three wishes.
> My three wishes came true all in one—you mom;
> someone who comforted and cared for me, wrong or
> right—
> You are the dusk of my days and my nights' dawns, and
> it is was your love that allowed me to sleep at night!
> I am sorry for the things I have said; unfortunately, the
> timing for my apologies has come too late—
> I wish you can awake and see my sorrow and know
> your being you was never a mistake!
> Plates hold food, dams hold water, but my heart will
> hold you forever and ever—
> As I hold your limp body, I damn the heavenly
> Father for taking you somewhere better.
> I will always keep your letters and my promise to make

sure the family stays intact—

In fact, I will seek the happiness you wanted for me

since I now have a reason to be sent back!"

After watching their brother cry, the siblings join Das, and together, they hold their mother's lifeless body, lying with her eyes still open. Following a moment's stare into her beautiful brown eyes, Das gently swipes his hands over them, closing them shut. Afterwards, he looks up at the medical professionals with his sagged eyes and bruised face. The staff lowers their heads. To allow the family a moment alone, the medical team leaves.

"What now, Das?" Kristoffe asks.

"Ye—yeah! What now?" Missilia cries.

"I do not know. For once in my life, I am unable to think."

Ten minutes after being alone, the family is interrupted by the return of two nurses.

"I need everyone to move aside," utters the taller and darker of the two nurses, "so we can make necessary preparations for your mother's body."

"What preparations must you make, she's already gone!" Das confronts.

The nurse responds with an awkward smile then asks her colleague to help her push the bed into the hall.

As the two nurses roll the recently deceased, woman's deathbed toward the doorway, each family member's eyes follow until the bed disappears into the hall. Shortly after the nurses' exit, the doctor pokes his head in the room.

"Monsieur Treymone! If you will, please come with me."

"What's wrong?" Das cries.

"Please, come with me."

Das leaves the family and meets with the doctor in the hall.

"Monsieur Treymone."

"Please, call me Das. No one except business acquaintances and law enforcement calls me by my last name."

"Well, Das. I know this is a difficult time for you right now, but as your being the oldest, there is a decision you must make."

"What kind of decision?"

"I need you to tell me whether you want to have your mother's body cremated or prepared for a traditional ceremony."

Das stares at the doctor with rage but doesn't respond.

"I understand the level of your grief," the doctor sympathizes, "yet, if you do not choose, your mother's body will be cremated!"

After pondering the doctor's words for a brief moment, Das calls his brothers and sisters into the hall. As they all line up, Das asks the doctor to ask the family the same question he asked him. The doctor squints at Das then turns his focus to the four siblings.

"I know this is a difficult time for all of you," the doctor says with sorrow, "but I need your choice of cremation or traditional burial service for your mother."

Each brother and sister directs their attention to Das, hoping he will answer. Das stares at each sibling briefly then looks at the doctor.

"Doctor," Das utters, "it is our wish to have our mother buried. Cost will not be a problem. Just assure me that you'll prepare the finest services for her."

"Will do. Do you have any other questions for me?"

"When and where will my mother's funeral service take place?"

"A week from today. Don't worry about travel, I will send someone for your family the morning of. Anything else?"

"No!"

"In that case, please have a safe journey home."

"Thank you."

The group of brothers and sisters marches to the whining hurt playing deep from within their hearts and minds towards the hospital's exit. After reaching Das's and Kristoffe's carriage, each sibling cries on one another's shoulder. Following an array of hugs and comforting words, the family boards its transport. Sighs, cries and tears replaces conversation as the motherless team heads towards Das's and Kristoffe's home.

When the family arrives to the house, each sibling enters without saying anything to each other. As they gather in the living room, Kristoffe lights five candles and hands one to each brother and sister, keeping one for himself. For the first time since their youth, the group kneels, holds hands and prays to the Lord. Thereafter, they speak about the fun things they experienced with their mother. As usual, Das takes the floor.

> "I can recall a time when mother and I would talk of
> accomplishing great deeds—
> She was a woman that had a huge imagination and
> prayed often for the growth of her planted seeds.
> I loved to watch her dance because she thought she
> knew of the up-to-date dance steps—
> She would have me laughing all day until I cried
> and until I ran out of breath!
> She was the definition of a friend even though her own
> sorrows brought her grief—
> Always speaking of happiness even when hard times
> would not bring her relief!
> I pray she be in peace with the best man anyone could
> ever have or ask for—
> Whenever I stare at the stars, I pray for the opportunity
> to see her through heaven's glass doors."

Das takes a seat on the sofa. Kristoffe stands and says a few words.

> "Even though we had to grow mainly on survival
> it was our mother's strength we endured—
> Of course she spoke of being weak, but spiritually
> she was our guide and mentor!"

Kristoffe allows De Ano the opportunity to take his place in front of the family then returns to his seat.

> "I was filled with rage and hate with both parents
> until mother tried to be my friend—
> Although the tides of our past washed ashore distaste,
> she never judged me for my sins!
> Strength depends on whoever has the fight and gall to
> stand to the jury of his or her own heart—
> Mother gave to me her undying love that even death

cannot ever tear apart!"

Usually the quietest of the family, Missilia takes her position in front of the group.

> "I've cried too much to speak in long terms, so I'll be
> brief and from my heart—
> Until I was reunited with our mother, the path I
> walked was so gruesome and so dark.
> I am happy to say I was able to meet her again, not
> only as my mother, but as my friend—
> Mother, if you are listening, pay attention to what my
> heart says over my mute silence."

Last, but not least, Amecca speaks her feelings.

> "I journeyed with a woman similar to myself in the
> respects of attitude, physique and choices—
> She always was there to protect me from my nightmares
> and all of those mysterious voices!
> I came to know her as a woman who went through
> so many obstacles to reach knowing herself—
> Little did mother know, her time with us was valuable,
> and it was an abundance of wealth!"

Following each sibling's heartfelt words, the family continues to talk in great lengths while drinking wine. Exhausted from crying and laughing and feeling partially intoxicated, everyone falls asleep in the area in which they sit. Das and Kristoffe lie next to each other on the floor; the other three lay on the couch, cuddling like a family of bears.

Very early in the morning, in complete darkness, Das awakes from a touch on his shoulder. His eyes open to a beautiful image of a woman that looks like his mother. With the belief that he is still intoxicated, Das shakes his head only to be given a clearer sight of the ghostly belle. The apparition waves him toward the stairs and tells him to remain quiet. Although in disbelief, Das creeps up the stairs behind the image and follows it into his room. They both take a seat on his bed. Somewhat frightened, absolutely nervous and lethargic, Das rubs his eyes then whispers.

He Speaks

>"This must be a dream for I know my mother is
>deceased and, with these hands I held her body—
>This moment now cannot be true for it is impossible
>for anyone to die then return to life!"

>Hair pulled back and dressed in a pure white gown, the
>image stares deeply into Das's eyes.

She Answers

>"I was allowed to come here to let you know that I did
>hear your empathetic words and apologies—
>I wanted to tell you that I am so proud that you decided
>to take care of the family!
>I read your mind and your heart and know there is one
>who you love and woe for—
>Your job is complete, owing nothing to anyone;
>therefore, go to her who you so longed for.
>Listen, my son, don't worry about me for I am in the
>best hands and can finally live free—
>I escaped the body, which imprisoned me and will
>never again feel trapped in captivity!
>Many actions were taken and many words were spoken
>that hurt, yet, Das, I understand—
>I know you have been dishonest with many women;
>nevertheless, I know you're now a wonderful man.
>I remember your dear former fiancée, Calia, and how
>you two didn't fit each other—
>Two things happened in that relationship, my son; you
>were in search of yourself and couldn't teach each
>other! I am not a therapist on relationships, but I do
>know my child whether or not you decide to believe
>me—

I ask you of this woman on your mind that deserves
such a great man and his feelings?"

Das stares at the apparition and hesitates to talk. Suddenly, the words flow from his lips like water through a broken faucet.

He Speaks

"Mother, I grew to know a woman that is for me and I
know I am for her—
When I received word for me to return home, I again
became so angry and so hurt!
I must admit, I hesitated to come, and now that I'm
here, I am happy with my decision—
It is interesting how Janicah knew I would be;
therefore, she allowed us this intermission.
As you know, I can speak with a tongue that can cut
almost anything; I believe I've cut her—
It was my natural reflex to speak when feeling cornered,
but mother, I do love her!"

She Answers

"You have granted many of my wishes so I say
the time has come for you to grant your own—
If it is her heart that you want, then it should be her
heart you should call your home!
I understand you want to spend time with the family
until my body is placed securely in the ground—
But promise me when this moment has pass, you'll
leave here and go to a woman who awaits you now!"

To the sound of her brother's voice, Amecca springs up then creeps up the stairs, tiptoeing towards his room. Remaining out of sight, she peeps through the crack of the door and sees Das sitting alone on the corner of his bed. As Das continues to talk, she continues to listen.

He Speaks

119

> "I have kept a secret from you mother that I wish to
> tell you about now—
> I killed the man responsible for the way I'm bruised
> and, for that, I cannot smile!
> This only happened a week ago, so your letter came
> at the perfect moment—
> Even though I was willing to stand to my persecution,
> Janicah wanted my atonement!
> This dilemma has my mind fluttered with worry and
> questions of how I can go back—
> Without bringing death upon myself or war on Janicah;
> Mother how do I go back?"

She Answers

> "The answer to any question is usually found in the
> mind and lips of the one who asks it—
> I cannot provide an answer to that one for it is you
> who must deal with what may happen.
> I must go now for my time with you have gone beyond
> the allotment that I was given—
> We have conversed at great lengths and exchanged
> some mental hugs and intellectual kisses!
> Regardless of the decisions you make in life, I will
> watch over you and help you—
> For a person who doesn't enjoy gambling, you have
> played well the hand life has dealt you!"

Amecca storms into Das's room and asks him with whom is he
speaking. Slightly baffled, Das tells her about his visit with their
mother. A concern expression crosses Amecca's face. Her mouth
drops open. "Don't play like that, Das!" she lashes. Das tells her
never mind then lies down. Unable to hold her tongue, Amecca
makes Das aware of her knowing about the murder in Santa Lucia.
Das tells his agitated sister to sit on the bed then tells her the entire
story. Following the story, Amecca forbids Das's seeing Janicah
again. Although he listens, Das kisses Amecca on the forehead and
orders her to go to sleep. Amecca refuses then tells him that if he

leaves Dalay he may be killed. As his sister rambles, Das turns onto his side and waits for her to be quiet. When she does, he speaks.

He Speaks

> "Understand and listen to the speeches the wind
> make before it decides to blow—
> Bellowing and howling at anyone in its path; those who
> decide to stay become victims of the cold!
> If I was to stay in this wind of concealment and
> unhappiness, it will be I who will languish—
> I will stay for a month at the most, then I will say
> good ridden to this anguish."

She Answers

> "I have lost a mother and will lose a brother if
> he adjourns to suicide—
> That is what they call a death when an individual
> decides to take his or her own life!"

He Speaks

> "Death will come whether I am sleeping or walking; it
> doesn't care about time or even love—
> It doesn't care that I am a man in search of happiness
> nor does it care that you are a woman!
> However, it knows that it has the key to any door and
> has strength to kill and command fleets—
> It can breach contracts, and cannot be sued by a mob
> of an angry twelve, sitting in court seats!
> So I say this to you, Amecca, I want to accomplish what
> I haven't and that's to feel wanted and loved—
> The opportunity is there as long as I am willing to
> make the journey; therefore, I'll soon be gone!"

She Answers

> "I can only pray when you do leave, the hands of God
> will push away all evildoers—

> That they be skewered by their methods of torture and
> realize that they are nothing more than losers!"

He Speaks

> "Sister, let's not quarrel anymore about this for
> it does neither one of us justice—
> Let us sleep now so tomorrow we can ready our
> minds and prepare for mother's funeral service!"

Following that night of frustration, Amecca and Das falls asleep. Late the following morning, each brother and sister go his and her own direction only to meet again in a week. Prior to attending the funeral, the siblings meet at Das's home then ride together to the service. There, at the site, everyone exchange cries and hugs. When the ceremony ends, the group disperses and continues living his and her life, talking to each other periodically. Fortunately, the bond between the siblings grows stronger like never before.

9
Ready to leave

It's been a month since Das and his siblings buried their mother and, in the interim, Das receives no response from the two letters he wrote Janicah. Afraid at the thought something has happened to her, he decides to return to Santa Lucia. He sends for the family then calls a meeting at his home. Once the family arrives, he asks everyone to take a seat in the living room. The group waits with anticipation. Finally, after a few sighs, Das informs the family of his leaving and that his heart is no longer in Dalay; it's in Santa Lucia. Missilia's and Amecca's eyes fill with tears; Kristoffe and DeAno lower their heads. Fed up with the discussion, Amecca quickly rises from the chair and pulls out a letter from her pocket, holding it in the air. "Is this reason you want to return, Das? Everyone, this letter is from Janicah— the woman responsible for our brother's anguish!"

At the sight of the letter, Das leaps from the sofa. "How dare you interfere with my life, Amecca?" he questions. Following a devilish smirk, Amecca crumbles the sheet in her palm then tosses it to her infuriated brother.

"How did you attain this without my knowledge, Amecca?"

"Quite simple, actually. It was delivered the morning of our mother's funeral service. I told the mail carrier that I will give it to you, but as you can see, I didn't. So while you were in the bathroom, freshening up, I put it in my purse with the hopes you would forget about this dame."

"You had no right to interfere with my life!"

"I have every right to protect a love one!"

For approximately ten minutes, the brother and sister feud over Janicah's letter and Das's decision to return to Santa Lucia.

"I hope you would forget about her, Das." Amecca concludes sadly.

Tired from arguing, Das reads the letter. Disrespectfully, Amecca threatens to tell the family about what she had overheard the night of their mother's death. Immediately, Das stops reading in mid-sentence and stares at his sister. Full of unstable emotions and sorrow, Amecca stands center of the living room and bellows all she overheard that ill-fated night. Kristoffe and De Ano look at their older brother with inquisition. Amecca's voice elevates with each thought of her brother possibly being killed, resulting from his actions over a month ago.

Unable to hear himself think, Das sits down and tries to shut out the commotion. His face sags with despondency. Noticing her brother is stressed, Missilia gives Das a hug and tells him to follow his heart. In turn, Das nods and smiles only to receive a puncturing glare from Amecca. No longer filled with animosity, Das calmly approaches Amecca and tries to reason with her.

He Speaks

> "The woman who I call sister and friend now
> treats me as if I'm her foe—
> Why must you close the door on my destiny, which
> is the only future that I know?
> Be jolly for me for I have not known any happiness
> in these years I've existed—
> Death has no detours, so eventually each road will
> surely come to its end!"

She Answers

> "I find it funny how men are ordained the strongest
> by God, yet, they're the simplest on earth—
> In this game of havoc, tragedy has thrown a pitch
> and you're nearly rounding first!
> If you want to enact a nightmare I once dreamt, I
> say to you be my guest—
> Although you and I are of the same blood and flesh, it's
> best you follow the beating concealed by your chest."

He Speaks

> "I assure you, my fair sister, that I am only afraid
> of conjectures and uncertainty—
> It's a burden to me if I don't go where Janicah is,
> and that has already began to murder me!
> Whether I die in the flesh or in spirit, the outcome

will unfortunately be the same—
It will not be the rain that will drench me, but
it will be my emotional pains.
I came back here under certain circumstances; however,
it is a must I again leave—
I came to see each of you on a disturbing day;
nevertheless, it pleases me to see your well-being."

She Answers

"My trying to convince you to stay is not working;
therefore, it is a must that I leave you with my love—
If you should need us to come to you, be sure you send
for us whenever and no matter what!"

Amecca, DeAno and Missilia give Das a group hug. As they walk towards the door, they look at their brother as if it would be their last time seeing him. Softly, Missilia closes the door following her exit.

Torn between love and hate for his brother, Kristoffe remains seated and quiet. Das looks at him for his blessing. Reluctantly, Kristoffe nods.

"Kristoffe, I am willing to stay for another week and nothing longer."

"That's a week longer than I had expected!"

"Well, let's make the best of it, shall we?"

"Let's…"

For the rest of the day and the next to come, Das and Kristoffe spend time with each other. The two brothers visit the heart of Dalay, speak of memories past and have lunches and dinners at their favorite eateries. To the come of nights, the two brothers return home, finishing the evenings like so many times before—wine drinking, jokes and card play.

Three mornings following Das's decision to leave, early morning knocks awakens Kristoffe from his hibernation. Tired and groggily from drinking the night previous, he slides on his slippers then staggers into his brother's room.

"Das, are you awake?"

"No! Go away!"

"Fine. I'll be the better of us and see who is at the door!"

"Go ahead and do that. It's probably someone for you anyway!"

Kristoffe throws a sock at Das's head then walks cautiously down the steps. When he opens the door, his eyes widen at a beautiful, five-foot-five, fair skin young women who he hadn't seen in years.

"Calia Morrey! What brings my brother's former fiancée to our home?"

"Hello to you, too, Kristoffe. Is your brother available?"

"He's upstairs sleeping. He wouldn't want to see you though!"

"That may be true, but let's just see."

"How would we do that if I do not choose to let you in?"

"Kristoffe, it's me—your favorite, remember?"

"You were before you broke my brother's heart!"

"That was two years ago!"

"That it was—still he suffers."

"I'm sure he does as I still do. May I come in now?"

"You may, but don't say I didn't warn you."

Kristoffe directs Calia to the sofa.

"Can I get you something to drink, Calia?"

"I'm fine. I won't be here long."

"I was only asking to be nice. Wait here as I attempt to get my brother."

Kristoffe darts up the stairs and storms into his brother's room.

"Das!"

"What?"

"There's someone here to see you!"

"Whom?"

"Go downstairs and see for yourself!"

Das throws on his robe then frowns at Kristoffe who stands before him with a devious smile. Afterwards, he hustles down the stairs. When he enters the living room, he becomes partially bothered. Refraining from saying anything profane, he takes a seat next to his former lover.

He Speaks

"To what degree do I owe this visit from a woman
who left me baffled and scarred?
The one who I had arrangements to marry only to
become a memory thus far!
It took the blessing of time for me to tackle the anguish
I encountered when you and I parted—
Five years we spent as a unit and with a change of
hand, I was discarded!"

She Answers

"Das, I did not come here to argue but to ask
you stay and not leave—
I received word from your sister, and I immediately
came like lightning speed!
Let's not point fingers of right or wrongs for we both
shared the same grief—
I spent five years as your woman, and I now come to
you as a friend in need.
Time has allowed me to see what's important and
what's unimportant to my existence—
I knew if you were to see me again, I would have to
deal with a lot of frustration and resistance!"

He Speaks

"My penguin, who I use to hold dearer than my
sister's child, why now?
When I didn't hear from you again, I had to learn to
get over you the only way I knew how!
I am sure you have found a man who is more
compatible to you than I ever could be—

You must have traveled long to get here and that alone
says you must still adore me!
Given the day when I cried streams on my pillow, I
would be happy to see you—
Now that I know this is a plot to have me stay, any
pleasing words from your lips will stop me from
believing you. I see through this plan developed by the
hands of my sister, but trust me it won't work—
If you were to walk out on me this time, I must tell
you that this time, it won't hurt!"

She Answers

"You know the happiest time that I've ever spent with
you was when we didn't argue—
Our constant arguing burdened me so much that I was
starting to lose myself and asked who were you.
I never once questioned if you were a man, but asked
were you really in love with me—
When you decided to cheat on me, it hurt worse than
anything that could've happened to me!
Although we were only together for a few months when
it happened, you waited a year to tell—
It was at that moment I knew the love I had for you
would no longer succeed, yet fail!
I stayed with you, not because I was afraid to leave, but
to see how great you really were—
I came to realize that you had to go find out what type
of man you really, really were!
You said anything I speak of a pleasant manner will be
of a plan to imprison you—
The biggest problem we shared together was not our
fights, it was the stubbornness that christened you!
I did not come to speak of reasons to stay or reasons to
leave for I want what you want—
Your sister spoke in length that something was going to
happen to you, so I decided to come.
While we were apart, I've been festered with idiots and

asses who don't truly know women—
I must say you always had a way with our species and
were able to grow immune to our emotional venom.
I know your leaving is for a sensational woman who
sparkles like sand on a dry beach—
Each day that pass, I pray that you and I would grow
friendly and become at least within an arms reach!
Today, I want to say sorry for a break up that left you
and I not as foes nor as friends—
Before something was to happen to one of us, I come to
you today and hope we can make amends!"

He Speaks

"When I finally became that man you deserved
it was you who turned to lies and deceit—
I knew it had to be a man that filled your head with
the ignorant thoughts of how to cheat!
In our relationship, I must agree, I spoke sharply, but I
did not leave you for another—
My regret was that I asked God to change me into a
good man for you that caused me to suffer.
Did I make mistakes? Yes! Have I done wrong? Of
course!
But to leave you was not an option—
I remember when I was going through unstable
emotions I asked you to leave, yet you chose not to.
Nothing could have hurt me the way your actions cut
me, then you left the knife in my heart—
Now that I am the man I should be, I am blessed with
one who loves me for each and every part.
You see, Calia, the wind blew away the remains of you
in my mind and carried to me a promise—
When the storm comes, the residue memories of us will
be washed away and I will be granted my wish!
Well, the storm has passed, the promise has been
fulfilled and the wish has come true—

She is awaiting my arrival soon; therefore, I will depart
here within two days then catch the train at noon!"

She Answers

"Das, I have always been in love with you and hope one
day you will truly believe that—
I felt like I wasn't your lady but a fellow soldier in a
war having to be prepared for combat!
When you asked me to marry you, I was made the
happiest woman on this tiny earth—
Then I came to the realization that it wasn't your heart
asking, it was your feelings of incompleteness and hurt!
I recited the words you wrote to me on our first
anniversary even though I ripped it up—
I pieced it back together when I satisfied the urge of
knowing you've been with another woman."

Calia motions to her feet then kneels before Das, placing a hand
on his knee and looking him directly in his eyes. Das frowns at her
action, yet he keeps his peace. Surprisingly, Calia recites the letter
Das had written her many years ago.

"Here I stand one year from being with a woman I can
journey throughout eternity—
The one who possess the strength of God's finger and
who is the definition of serenity.
Warmth blankets the winter whenever she smiles and
autumn rains cease whenever she speaks—
Clouds disperse when she walks, letting through the sun
that strengthens the emotionally weak!
Each day is a blessing when I am able to see her, and
each moment is an opportunity to say three words—
I will forever love the person that is beside me on this
one year, and I will never, ever leave her!"

He Speaks

"I am surprised that you could remember such words
when I didn't believe you cared—
Why did you quit on me? Why did you think it was best
that you went elsewhere?
I remember the moment that put a foul taste in my
mouth and allowed the clouds to cover my house—
When I came to visit an exquisite woman, it turned out
to be she was with a different man on the couch!"

She Answers

"I didn't know who I was, but I did know my friends'
influences played a major role—
Not to blame it on anyone particular; I needed to find
myself when I had no direction to go!
I made you my life, wanted to be your wife, and wanted
to bear a child from your nightly works—
We spent nearly five years together and every moment
we grew apart, I lived every awaiting moment confused
and hurt!"

Calia rises from the floor and signals Das of her ready to leave.
Thoughts of his past with Calia occupy his mind. Sadden by his
brief reminiscing, Das raises from the sofa. Hesitantly, he grabs
Calia by the hand and escorts his former lover to the door.

He Speaks

"I know I have spoken to you with the intent to demean
you; thus, I ask you for your mercy—
I cannot fight the thought that I still love you and can't
believe that today, we talked without blame or cursing.
Now, I will allow you to leave, knowing I will always
love you for you will forever be my penguin—
Who knows, maybe in this life or another, you and I
will experience the feeling of being together again."

Das opens the door. "I hope this will not be the last time I see
that beautiful smile," Calia utters. "I assure you, it won't be," Das
smiles. As the two, former lovers hug, Calia kisses the right side

of Das's neck. "I will always love you Das," she whispers in his right ear. As if terrified, Das quickly pushes Calia arm-length away. Following a deep and surprised stare, and a small smile, Calia turns away. As she steps away, Das grabs her by the hand and brings her to his bosom, holding her tight and resting his chin on the top of her head.

"I can't let go just yet," Das says softly as good memories of the two continue to parade through his mind.

While caught up in the moment of fond memories, stemming from their relationship, Das kisses Calia on her forehead. In turn, she looks up at Das's awkward smile then closes the door, kissing her former fiancé on his lips. Unfortunately, the thought of Janicah becomes lost between Das's present feelings for Calia.

Under an umbrella of silence, the two hormone-driven, ex-lovers' eyes asks consent.

"Das," Calia calls seductively, "I want to make love to you as if this were our first time. If you were to fulfill my request, I will leave here a happy, complete woman!"

Somewhat honored, Das kisses Calia and gently nibbles her bottom lip. The uncontrollable groping begins.

In the heat of the lustful moment and, without regards to Kristoffe's sleeping, Das leads Calia to his bedroom. There, the two amorous individuals attack each other, savagely. In the midst of kissing and fondling Calia, Das removes her summer dress; she removes his robe. Both naked and filled with anticipation, the rubbing of each other's body continues. In a barbaric fashion, Das throws Calia face-down on the bed then inserts his erection into her moistened gap from behind. The two moan from the familiar delight. Following ten minutes of pounding Calia's opening, Das allows his sweaty partner the opportunity to straddle him. Calia's hip-thrusts and untamed bucking forces Das to bite his lip, trying to refrain from hollering with joy. Finally, at the end of an exhausting, thirty-minute, complete-body workout, the two reacquainted friends lay next to each other— exhausted and in disbelief. After regaining control of his breathing, Das directs Calia's head onto his chest and whispers.

He Speaks

> "It's been so long passed the time you and I had the
> opportunity to make love in this fashion—
> For so long I've wanted to relive the burning fires of
> your desires and re-experience your passion."

She Answers

> "Das, I want you to go to the woman who has your
> heart, but also take a piece of my soul with you—
> Each time I was in a different relationship, I cried at the
> fact I was no longer with you!
> Go and be merry and allow the journey to bring you
> smiles along with the ability to cherish—
> Be sure you send me a letter if you and her decide to
> come together as one flesh in marriage!"

He Speaks

> "I will take more than a piece of your soul when I
> leave; I will also take with me our memories—
> They will allow me to be a perfect man for Janicah,
> guiding me away from reliving my actions in history!
> I never stopped loving you even when I decided to not
> write; yet, I would've been there for you if you needed
> me—
> You have succeeded to becoming the friend I will
> always adore, and in turn, I will be yours for eternity!"

Das rises from the bed and grabs massage oil from his dresser,
leaving Calia lying bare-ass and relaxed. Upon his return, he takes
a seat on the edge of his bed, grabs Calia's left foot and sucks each
one of her flawless toes. Calia bursts with laughter from the tickling
sensation. "Stop," Calia giggles, "you're making me laugh!"
Following his massaging of Calia's back and legs, Das speaks.

He Speaks

> "The few times we discovered happiness, it was times
> like this one I loved and appreciated most—
> I know I brought you many burdens of guilt, but a smile
> comes to me due to this special moment…"

After a few hours of resting and talking about memories past, Calia rises from her relaxation and begins to get dressed. Das gawks as he puts on his robe. Following another passionate kiss, Das escorts Calia to the front door where the two converse briefly.

"I love you, Das!"

"I love you too," Das responds while hugging Calia close.

"Remember, my heart will forever beat for you!"

"As mine will forever keep you within!"

Calia ends the conversation with a kiss to Das's cheek. Holding the door wide-open, Das watches as Calia's coachman assists her into her carriage. Once she becomes situated, Das waves farewell. Joyfully, Calia returns the gesture; yet, a single tear glides down her cheek. Once the carriage sets in motion, Calia blows a kiss to Das then smiles as he motions to catch it. Soon, Calia and her coach becomes merely a passing moment in Das's life.

Saddened by fond memories of his past with his former lover, Das slowly closes the door, pondering his recent experience with Calia. Following a brief moment to himself, he scales the mountain of stairs then sways to the melodies of guilt into his room. While sitting on his bed, he mutters.

He Speaks

> "Temptation is definitely the most deadly of all sins
> that is known to man—
> I have indulged in a fantasy-like moment, and now, in
> this midst of confusion is where I stand!
> I have fulfilled a duty that wasn't mine to fulfill, but
> because of our past, I had a reason—
> I have ignored the thoughts of my Janicah and satisfied

an urge, which leaves me in treason!
Winter is the season in my heart; thus, the snowflakes
of emotions are falling—
I do not regret what I have done, though someone else
would find my acts appalling!
No longer should I stall in this climate where the dew
speaks to the morning sun—
I promised my heart that I will leave at the dawn of
when the next morning comes!"

As Das lived each day as he pleased, Janicah has patiently waited for his return. Since his departure, her days consisted of sitting in the house, reading, bathing and eating. The same day Das makes love to Calia, Janicah lies on her bed worrying whether he is safe.

She Answers

"It's nearing a month and a half since I talked to Das,
and here I lay on my bed thinking about a dream—
It seems that I should be out and about, freeing myself
from all this worry and thinking!
The hour is noon as I'm consuming tonic, alone,
wearing nothing more than my panties and my man's
shirt—
I have not received my period and believe that
I may be carrying a young boy or girl!
It was spring when Das came to me, and here it is the
beginning of a calm summer—
I am without anyone right now, crying at the possibility
I'm pregnant, filled with wonder!
I question whether he will return by next week, if not,
I'll write a letter stating my journeying in life alone—
I will rest my worry along with these tears, and allow
myself the wellness I need inside my own home!
While lions roam and roar, I will be the eagle that soars
over the rivers and the oceans—
No longer will I be held down by uncertainties and the
days of hoping—no more hurt emotions."

10

The Unpleasant Welcome

Das's day to return to Janicah has finally come. It is a warm morning while he awaits his train, comforted by his siblings. Following ten minutes of family discussion, the train to Santa Lucia arrives. First, Kristoffe hugs his brother, then De Ano, Missilia, and reluctantly, Amecca. "Amecca," Das whispers in his sister's ear, "sorrow not for my absence; yet smile for my eternal bliss!" Amecca nods her head then embraces her brother.

"Well, I'm off everyone," Das smiles. "Wish me luck in my new life."

"Be sure to come back and visit us," Missilia cries.

"Yes, older brother," Kristoffe follows. "Be sure to visit."

The group of siblings watches as their brother boards the train. After taking his seat, Das waves, refraining from crying. The saddened bunch mirrors his action, and within a couple of minutes, the train becomes only an outline in the distance. Following a group hug, Kristoffe accompanies his siblings to his coach. Filled with sadness, the lonely pack journeys to Kristoffe's home.

Head aching from crying, Das forces himself to sleep. Minutes of being in a deep slumber, he becomes subdued by a vision. His dream reveals to him his death—a vicious stabbing, which ends his life. In a cold sweat, Das awakes, heart beating tremendously, then stares out the window, thinking about his family. As his trip continues, he only sleeps an hour or two at a time.

On the evening of the sixth day of travel, Das and the other passengers arrive to the warmth of Santa Lucia— the village of Das's angel, Janicah. Politely, he allows the impatient travelers to fill the available coaches. Filled with happiness of being nearly to his queen, he sits on a bench and decides to wait for another coach. Alone at the train station, he is approached by two officers. One is well-built and very dark; the other slender and pale. Unfortunately, and little to Das's knowledge, these officers are the two friends of Danma Fierre who escaped his wrath.

"Had a long journey, friend?" asks the dark officer.

"Indeed it was, yet, it was nice, nonetheless."

The dark officer and Das continues to converse. However, the ghostly pale officer stands on Das's right. Feeling a little on edge, Das rises slowly to his feet as he continues to converse with the dark officer. Suddenly, the pale fellow throws his arm around Das's neck in a friendly fashion. Without warning, the friendly hug becomes a chokehold, forcing Das to hunch over. While Das fights for freedom, the dark officer thrusts his club into his stomach. On his knees in pain, Das is beaten savagely by the two officers. Each taking turns kicking and punching him. To end this display of indecent acts, the pale officer pulls out a dagger from his gear then jabs it into Das's side, whispering, "We're good friends of Danma Fierre. He may now rest knowing he has been avenged." Weakened by the blow, Das trembles as his blood flows from his side like a stream onto the asphalt. With his last bit of energy, he jumps to his feet and punches the pale officer in the eye. Out of breath from the lunge, Das drops to the ground like a sack of rocks. Quickly, the officers scurry away like rodents.

While lying on the ground with his blood streaming from his side, Das gasps for breath and attempts to stand. He fails. Following two more tries, his blood-soaked attire anchors him to the ground. Sadly, thoughts of his family and Janicah flash intermittently through his mind as he patiently awaits death. "Janicah, I'll always love you," he gasps.

Possessed to take an evening stroll, Janicah leaves the house unaware of what has happened to Das. At the start of her walk, a brisk wind nips at her uncovered flesh. Although the draft was bizarre, Janicah ignores it then journeys toward the ocean.

In the middle of her excursion, Janicah walks by the train station. A huge crowd whispering amongst itself captures her attention. Struck by curiosity, she finds it necessary to see the spectacle that has the crowd in awe. With all of her might, she fights through the wall of people until she reaches the front. Her eyes widen at the man lying on his stomach in a pool of blood. Little regard for her own clothes, Janicah kneels next to the man and calls for his attention. "Monsieur, can you hear me? Monsieur?" The mob hovers over her as she continues to speak to the unfortunate man. "Someone get help!" she yells. "What is wrong with all of you? Get help!" At the scream of a familiar voice, Das finds the strength to roll onto his back. Shocked by the man's face, Janicah cuffs Das's head. "What happened?" she cries. "What happened, Das?" As Das's eyes roll in the back of his head, he rambles.

He Speaks

> "In the rain of misfortune comes the sun of grief,
> melting the morning dew of happiness—
> I lay underneath the umbrella of chance, which shields
> me from the showers of complete blackness!
> Within the distance of my sight is the woman I came to
> know and will love even in death—
> In this time of winter's dawns and autumn's dusks, I
> am to be the cabbage pushed aside for no longer being
> fresh. I am called to God's desk for the answer to the
> question why I decided the path I chose to walk—
> I speak in whispers only to be heard by the fawn that
> gazes upon the heavens, watching the acrobatics of
> the hawk. Stalking me is a stranger dressed in black,
> wearing a matching cloak and awaiting the moment I
> collapse—
> I have escaped many traps, eradicated objectives, and
> here I lay horizontally like the lines found on road
> maps! Coming upon me is numbness, taking the feeling
> of my feet slowly away while gaining control of my
> legs—
> I sit restless like the hen that wants to play with the
> roosters, but she can't for she must tend to her eggs!"

A small spurt of blood seeps from Das's mouth as he tries to complete his words. Janicah takes her right sleeve and brushes it across her dying man's face.

As Janicah weeps, Das's eyes reveal the coming of his last breaths. Janicah slowly lifts her head and sees that an officer has arrived to the scene. Following his parting of the spectators, the officer gently places a hand on Janicah's shoulder and informs her that help is on its way. He also explains that Das's chances of surviving are slim. Unable to voice a reply, Janicah nods her head.

For respect of the fallen man and his lady, the officer orders the spectators to leave the premises. Once they disperse, he watches as Janicah cries, securing her man's head in her hands.

She Answers

> "I thought you had forgotten about me and wasn't
> certain that you would ever come back to me—
> As I sit here holding you, it's as if I'm trapped in a bad
> dream for I cannot believe this is happening.
> My Das, I beg that you attempt to survive this injustice
> that has been unfortunately brought upon you—
> I will not believe my fate was to give my love to a man
> only to have it taken away by this that was done to
> you!"

He Speaks

> "Gentle be the torture that has ripped through my flesh
> and released this massive amount of blood flow—
> The smile of the devil has darkened my days in ways no
> man should ever and never know!
> Astray is the direction I travel where the destination is a
> corner occupied by the aroma of regret—
> I am a slave in the field of wickedness, working in
> this warm climate, which causes my exhaustion and
> my body to sweat. I have been challenged by time, the
> champion that stands victorious over each and every
> one of its enemies—
> I have been defeated by its accomplice named
> incompetence; thus I've been left here to die, heavily
> breathing. I sit in the tears of the crying clouds and the
> breath of the screaming winds that yells with fury—
> I look up at the smiles of a million souls, flickering
> during the sleep of the most precious of Lord's jewelry!
> I dreamt of being a beach that provides miles of soft
> sand for those whom seek peace and relaxation—
> Instead I am the high tide, which brings ample amounts
> of sea debris, causing a chaotic evacuation!"

Janicah shifts her position and continues to secure Das's head between her lap and her hands. Das's eyes roll aimlessly around, nearly closing. Worried and panicked, Janicah shakes him gently, slapping him into coherency. Struggling for life, Das looks at her with his dilated pupils and attempts to speak. "Jah-ni-cah!" he gasps. Eyes swollen from crying, Janicah whispers a series of hushes and tells Das he needs to save his strength.

She Answers

> "Speak no more for you need your strength to climb
> this mountain that is set before you—
> I assure you I will not let you leave my grasps
> regardless of whom or what may come for you!
> Breathe Das! Breathe! I need you to fight this battle that
> wants to claim your victory—
> I believe I am with a seed fertilized by your loins, so do
> not leave me here in misery!"

Das's eyes widen to Janicah's possibility of being pregnant. He whimpers like an injured pup and adjusts himself in Janicah's arms.

He Speaks

> "The pain of every man's soul is not due to what he has,
> but what he doesn't possess—
> The emptiness of my heart has been filled, so it will be
> easier for me to finally rest.
> The greatest gift to any man is the love of a woman
> who is so wholesome and so beautiful—
> I love every square inch of your mind, every follicle on
> your body, your every word and cuticle.
> You are possibly with our child who may never get to
> know the touch or words of its father—
> I am dying, my sweet Janicah, from the wound of
> revenge that makes my blood flow like water!
> I flutter like the otter in this sea of foul deeds,
> swimming to the slimy shore of dismay—

Never in the most horrible of my nightmares I could
have dreamt to spend time with you in this way!"

Janicah bends forward and kisses Das on the forehead.

She Answers

"I wish I could go back in time and leave with you on
your journey to see your mother—
To be able to go back and change your mind about
coming back here and end this that makes you suffer!
I look at the tears in your eyes and wish I were laying
here in your arms, awaiting my last breath—
The pain of my wound would be healed by the touch of
a medicated kiss from your lips to my head.
I've read your letters and kept them underneath the
pillow, which comforts me while I dreamt of us—
Uniting us as one under oath in the Lord's name, living
merry with no burdens or anything strenuous!
I beg that you don't leave me again for this time I may
not be able to proceed in a forward direction—
My days will consist of meaningless smiles; the nights
will permit the frowns that will bring wrinkles to my
complexion!"

Following Janicah's last word, a team of men in white suits,
holding black bags and stethoscopes arrive at the scene. After talking
to the officer, they rush to Janicah and the nearly decease man. From
the group of three medical persons, one of the gentlemen introduces
himself to Janicah. "Madame, I'm Dr. William Obknock. We need
you to move so we can examine the patient." Janicah softly places
Das's head on the cement then eases to her feet, blood dripping from
her dress and hands.

While examining Das, Dr. Obknock asks Janicah her relation to
the fallen fellow. Without hesitation she replies, "He's my husband!"
Afterwards, she stands over the medical team, waiting impatiently
the outcome.

As the team cuts open Das's shirt, Janicah stares at the blood on
her hands then drops to her knees, praying for a miracle.

"Lord, the foothills of life are not solid and neither was
my faith to love a man again—
You once answered my prayer that I would hold dearest
one who is special, but he is here dying!
I beg that you bring life back to the him I want to marry
and to grow old with—
For You are Master of all things mighty and diminutive;
therefore, I know you have the power to do this!"

Janicah rises from her knees and waits impatiently for the
medical team to finish its duty. Quietly she stands a few feet away
from the team's whispers and Das's gasps for air. Suddenly, she hears
a faint voice calling her name. "Jah-ni-cah!" She looks around. No
one except the officer is nearby. Again, she hears the hoarse calling.
"Jah-ni-cah!" Finally, it dawns on her. The whining calls are from
Das. Gloom in her eyes, Janicah looks at Dr. Obknock, awaiting
his approval to let her come to her dying man. Once on his feet, Dr.
Obknock waves Janicah over.

"Madame, I think this young man needs to talk to you."

"Thank you, doctor."

Filled with hopelessness, Dr. Obknock and his team form a
huddle away from the unfortunate couple to discuss Das's irreversible
condition. Periodically, Dr. Obknock looks at the couple.

As the medical staff speaks among itself, Janicah kneels next to
her man and rubs his pale cheeks. With his last bit of wind, Das says
his final words.

He Speaks

"I never knew of a man who could love and be loved
until you showed him to me—
I never knew that this world of unsightly actions and
hate could have someone with so much overall beauty!
The strength that is left in this body is being used to
keep my eyes open to see your face—
It is this sight I want to keep when darkness rolls over
the hills and when death takes the stage!
My age is young, yet, my heart is mature from the
nurture of a woman I know as my Queen Janicah—

Just know I will everlastingly be with you, so cry no
more at the thought I may be gone forever!
I will say I love you now and multiply it by the number
of stars in the heavens, so please don't forget—
Even though I lay here, prepared to leave this earth in
your hands, all that came from loving you, I have no
regrets!"

She Answers

"Damn you if you die on me for I cannot forgive you in
a million years the sun burn—
Make a u-turn from the path that wants to take you
further from me; I command you to stand firm!"

Janicah awaits a response; none is given. She shakes Das by
his shoulders only to receive no reaction. Although his eyes are
fixated on her, his body remains motionless. "No!" Janicah screams.
"Lord, not my Das!" To Janicah's outburst, Dr. Obknock leaves his
congregation then places a hand on Janicah's shoulder, explaining
his team did all they could do. In turn, Janicah grabs his hand and
squeezes it with all her might, trying to ease some of her own pain.

"Young lady, what is it you would like to do at this moment?"
asks Dr. Obknock.

"I shall hold him as long as I am able," Janicah responds sadly.

"Very well," Dr. Obknock slowly withdraws his hand. "You may
hold him for a little while. I will have one of my men fetch the burial
wagon."

Dr. Obknock orders his crew to go to the hospital and return with
the burial wagon. Quietly, he and the officer wait with Janicah who
continues to cry over Das's body. Following three hours, the coffin
wagon stops next to the bloody scene.

"Madame," Dr. Obknock interrupts Janicah's sobbing, "the time
has come to let go!"

"Must I?"

"Sadly to say, yes. However, you are welcome to accompany us
to the morgue." "I will come," Janicah replies, watching sorrowfully
as two men place Das's body carefully into the rear of the wagon.

Unable to control her tear flow, Janicah grabs Das's suitcase then joins the doctor and his team on the coach.

While traveling to the mortuary, in the midst of broken branches made by the crushing wagon wheels, Janicah closes her eyes and thinks of memories past. She recalls the first day Das arrives at her doorstep. As she smiles at the handsome man with big brown eyes and his smooth, bronze complexion, tears flow even harder. The vivid vision seems as if it were yesterday. Slowly, she reaches for her man's hand then escorts him to the sofa. Sadly, she replays each word, each action, and every tear of that moment. Eyes still closed, she utters.

> "Without you I am only a powder bonded by clay and
> shaped by running shame and tears—
> The vision of my sights were opaque and when you
> came to me my sights became crystal clear.
> I want to be the sun you awake to and the moon that
> allows you to peacefully sleep—
> To be the rays of sunshine that warms your body and
> the tingle you feel when goose bumps creep.
> I want to be the blue sky you look abroad, and the floors
> that hold the weight of your burdens—
> When peeping Toms look through your windows and
> disrespect your privacy, I want to be your curtains!
> I want to be the strength when your muscles become
> tired and when your body becomes restless and ill—
> To be the 360 degrees of your circle, and the queen
> who'll carry out every order of your will!
> I want to be the sheets that wrap your body and the
> pillow that aids you in your nights' comfort—
> To be the autumn's rain that washes away calamity and
> discontent only to bring you the joys of summer!
> Now I am the runner, sprinting in the direction of
> misfortune into the forest of uncertainty and malice—
> My God-crafted hands hold the memories of a man due
> to the malicious acts Satan had time to practice.
> I am only an actress role-playing a helpless but strong
> woman in this film of disturbed scenes—

The herds of good emotions have left the pasture of my
heart; unfortunately, the grass is no longer green!"

After traveling for half an hour, the wagon arrives at the
mortuary. Two medics remove Das's body from the wagon then
brings it inside. Before Dr. Obknock and Janicah follow, the doctor
grabs the miserable woman's attention.

"Young lady, should I have the mortician prepare the body for a
traditional service or a cremation?"

Janicah ignores the doctor then follows the other men into the
mortuary. Slightly agitated from being ignored, the doctor catches
up with Janicah.

"Madame, I know the pains you feel, but I need a decision
now!"

Janicah stops in mid stride and looks at the doctor with fury. Her
glare motivates the doctor to take a step back. As the doctor waits
for an answer, he finally receives one.

"I do not want to have his body in the soil that grows
hate and gives birth to maggots—
I would rather jar his ashes and take him with me so I
can grant his wish to be free in the wind!
I say get the torch and everything else necessary to burn
this body, ready to lay on fagots—
I will spread him amongst the breaths of the individuals
who participated in his tragic end!"

Dr. Obknock acknowledges with a head nod. Once he and
Janicah enter the massive, stone building, an ash-covered, old
man with white hair and a permanent squint approaches them. Dr.
Obknock greets the unusual fellow and explains to him the task at
hand. Following a headshake, the old man hobbles toward Janicah
and gives his condolences. Disgusted by the man's appearance,
Janicah quickly turns away. Not bothered by her rudeness, the
mortician grabs Janicah's feather-soft hands and rubs it with his
blistered and scabbed fingers. Filled with rage, Janicah snatches her
hand from the morticians grasps then urges him to do his duty. "Get
away from me," she hollers. "What reason do you have to speak to
me or touch me?" The mortician nods then smiles. Next, he orders

the men holding Das's body to put the decease on the eleven-foot, chain-operated bed. Once the mortician starts the fire the crowd watches in awe.

After fifteen minutes of waiting for the stove to get hot enough to singe even the devil's eye brows, the group watches as Das's body slowly slides headfirst into the fire-filled pit. At the stench of burning flesh, the medical team covers their noses and become filled with nausea as they watch Janicah inhale deeply. Afar off in the corner, the mortician smiles at his furnace and rubs his hands together as if he's a part of a sinister plot. Within minutes, Das's body disappears into the belly of the stove. Nearly suffocating from the nauseating smell of charred flesh, the medical team escapes the palace of disgusting fumes, holding their breath until outside. Against the wagon they inhale and relax. Yet, Janicah stays and continues to watch the flames salvage her man's body for the entire time it takes it to burn.

Once the ashes cool, the mortician scoops the remains into a clay jar then hands it to Janicah. She quickly brings the jar to her bosom, crying like a newborn child. The mortician, then, wraps an arm around Janicah's torso and escorts her to the wagon. "The Madame has all she needs," he utters to the team. "Make sure she gets home." Dr. Obknock assists the saddened dame onto the wagon then leaves the palace of brimstone. In a small voice he asks, "Young lady, where should we take you?" Janicah doesn't respond. The doctor asks once more. Compelled to answer, Janicah gives the doctor directions to her home. Hurt and filled with animosity, she whispers to Das's remains.

> "The joys of life are those we as humans look over and
> take for granted—
> I've been handed a blessing and, within a short time,
> it was taken from me!
> In this dry climate where the sun evaporates all that is
> wet, I sit here in dampness—
> How is it I could have everything I wanted only to be
> left standing with nothing?
> I wish I could spread you amongst the earth and have
> you grow as a field of roses—

Instead, I am sitting here holding your remains and all
the pains associated!
I ask that you come and take me from this prison of
fallacy once done when you wrote me—
If I speak with shallow words about this world, I do not
care whether it's right or inappropriate!"

Janicah closes her eyes and speaks to the Lord

"I dare not challenge the decision of the omnipotent,
but I ask why you took my Das—
I thought I found all that I could ever need; now I
realize I am nothing more than a child lost!
I begged you to send me someone I could hold and
grow grays in my hair with—
Someone I can talk to and hold and someone I can care
for and to share my life with!"

Janicah hears a quiet voice then feels a warm touch on her
stomach. Little does she know, the voice and touch is from an angel
acting on the behalf of God.

"I answered the prayer of my child by allowing her to
possess a fertilized egg—
Das will forever be a part of you in spirit; all I have
done was taken him in the flesh!
The hurdle of pain set before you is difficult to jump
over but I'll give you the strength—
Underneath your sorrow and your desires for more lays
abundance of happiness of immeasurable lengths!
Live merry, Janicah, for the sign of a new dawn is
present in your womb and awaits the time to shine—
I have created time so it can heal the wounds of your
lost, but understand Das will be with you at all times!"

Janicah sighs at the voice in her head then rubs her stomach.
After arriving home, Dr. Obknock escorts her to the door and
apologizes once again. Janicah looks at him with disgust and says
an array of rude lines.

"Save your apologies for you are called a doctor,
yet you cannot save a life—
If you want to apologize—apologize that I will forever
be in mourning and never become a wife!
Apologize for the length of time it took you and your
accomplices to arrive at the scene—
I apologize that your team of incompetent professionals
are only good at waking up and breathing!"

Dr. Obknock opens his mouth to challenge Janicah's harsh words, but he doesn't say anything. He realizes the amount of pain Janicah is experiencing and tells her to live merry. Realizing she was shrewd, Janicah apologizes to the doctor then gives him a hug. Happily, the doctor returns to his wagon, waiting for Janicah to enter her house. Before Janicah inserts her key into the keyhole, her mother opens the door. Worry flashes across her face, yet, disappears at her daughter's sad expression and bloodied dress. Silently, she leads Janicah inside. Assured that Janicah is safe, Dr. Obknock and his team roll into the evening.

As Janicah sits on the sofa, holding Das's ashes in her blood-soaked dress, she cries. Without words, her mother comforts her. Stricken with a headache, eyes swollen from crying, Janicah whispers to her fallen prince.

"I have been purposely lured into the arms of grief that
hold me as if I am its child—
I feel faint each time I stand, fatigue when I walk, and
locked jaw when I smile!
I am nothing more than a pebble tossed by the hands of
reality, skipping on the waves of fantasy—
The net of cruelty has captured my dreams and
sentenced them for life in its infirmity!"

Janicah removes the lid from the jar of ashes, staring at her man's remains. Two tears race down her face, landing on top of the powdery substance. After staring sadly into the jar, Janicah replaces the lid then places it onto the fireplace mantle. Weighed down by sadness, she staggers to her mother's comfort. Holding the sobbing young woman, Janicah's mother kisses her daughter's head, still consoling her daughter with quietness. Tired herself, Claire retires upstairs, leaving Janicah in the living room, anchored by her emotions. Overcome with a moment's strength, Janicah starts a fire in the fireplace then lies weeping on the floor. Soon she cries herself to sleep.

While Janicah sleeps, a warm, subtle breeze awakes her. Head heavy and aching, she slowly scans the dim, fire-lit room. Neither the window nor the door is open or ajar.

Assured that the living room is secure, Janicah returns to her rest; the image of Das stands over her.

He Speaks

> "I wish I could hold you as before, protecting you from
> every pain and every disturbance—
> I am here although you will never hear my voice or see
> me; however, know you'll fear no menaces!
> Sleep, my sweet, for your mourning for me will end
> sooner than your mind will ever know—
> I beg that you not curse my death for you will always
> possess my spirit and my soul!"

The image of Das lies next to Janicah, wrapping its arms around her torso. Still in a sound sleep, Janicah adjusts to the warmth which feels so familiar.

She Answers

> "It feels like you're still with me, though I know you
> are playing with the angels in heaven—
> This warmth that surrounds my body is the same I felt
> when we use to lay together, laughing!
> Within these ropes of life challenges and strings of
> loneliness, I am the lamb which is tangled—
> I'm sure you want me to love again, but I swear by our
> child's head I'll love no other man!"

Das kisses Janicah's neck then squeezes her tight. Afterwards, he places one of his ghostly hands on his woman's stomach, rubbing it in a circular motion.

Ellard Thomas

He Speaks

> "Gentle be the child who is protected by a womb of a
> woman filled with love and guidance—
> Never hiding like the coward who speaks with a foul
> tongue and conceals his face by the shadows!
> This is the seed of a tree planted in the finest of all soil
> available on this intriguing planet—
> You will be the rarest of God's gems—a diamond from
> His necklace of stars and pendants!
> I will be your eyes in the dark passages and the light
> needed to help you see—
> I know you cannot understand me now, but know inside
> of you is the strength of your mother and me!"

Janicah smiles, and the familiar warmth gives her peace
throughout the night. Arm around her waist, Das's image holds
Janicah until the morning.

Early the following morning, Janicah's eyes open slowly. She
stares at the window from her horizontal position, hesitating to sit
up. Following a long yawn, she stands to her feet then kisses the jar
of ashes. Standing before it, she whispers.

She Answers

> I know you want me to carry on my daily activities;
> yet I need you to tell me how—
> I'll bellow until my voice reaches the ears of those able
> to hear the words of a woman who is no longer proud!
> The clouds that send rain are my shrouds, hiding me
> from the warmth of the sun—
> I will try my hardest to live each day without you; I beg
> you aid me through day one!"

Overcome with hope, Janicah walks away from the jar, rushing
up the stairs into her room. Das follows. While in Janicah's room, Das
watches Janicah gather some clean clothes from her dresser drawer.
Satisfied with her selection, Janicah hurries into the bathroom and
runs a bath, sighing deeply between breaths. Das stands behind her.

Sitting on the side of the tub, Janicah cries as the tub fills up. After shutting off the water, she removes her garments then steps into the soothing, hot water. Trying to remove her mind from the particulars of the day previous, Janicah's mother knocks on the door.

"Are you okay, Nicah?"

"I'm fine," Janicah replies.

"Okay, Pumpkin. I just wanted to make sure!"

Janicah closes her eyes; Das stares from the toilet. Determined to touch Janicah, Das kneels next to the tub and goes through the motions of bathing his queen.

He Speaks

> "I sit next to a woman who has a mind of a general
> and a body of a goddess—
> She's a woman so modest, filled with strength and has
> the ability to control fleets with soft words.
> She is a moving picture where each movement says the
> minimum of a million words—
> She has a voice so gentle, but has a keen intellect that is
> sharper than a million swords.
> She is my umbilical cord, attaching me to life, the hand
> which continues to feed my soul—
> I am the mole traveling through the darkness of the
> earth in seek of the correct direction to go!
> Janicah is my mixture of gold, platinum and diamonds,
> and all others that are considered rarities—
> When deception covered my eyes, the kiss from her lips
> to my head brought to me a much needed clarity!"

The rising hairs on Janicah's neck force her to submerge deeper into the water. In disbelief that her man is gone, her eyes fill with mist. Das extends his left hand and tries to catch the tear from falling into the tub; unfortunately, the tear travels through his hand, splashing into the tub. Eyes on Janicah, he continues to speak.

> "Although I am free from the imprisonment of my
> physical being, I am still a serf—

151

Living in the chains of non-existence, bounded to the
memories that is the cause of my own torture!
I look at the moisture of my woman who breathes the
air that I cannot feel but can only see—
I sit next to this tub unseen by the eyes of my queen,
and still I will not ever think about leaving!
I breathe, but oxygen isn't what I inhale, it's the
imaginary flow of toxins within the air—
It's sad to know that my lady will never feel my rubbing
her feet, my kissing her head, or my fingers brushing
through her hair!
My only purpose here is to guide my woman through
the tunnels of sorrow and the paths of rapture—
To allow her the opportunity to complete the sentences
needed to finish this miserable, first chapter!
I fractured my opportunity of contentment when I left
her to frolic with my former sweet—
Only to return here and be murdered by the hands of
vengeful demons that sought their revenge and war
upon me."

Following her bath, Janicah exits the tub and wraps a towel
around her body. Afterwards, she walks through Das, moping into
her bedroom. Sadly, Das trails, watching as Janicah dry her legs then
the rest of her body. Spread naked amongst her bed, Janicah cries
out for Das.

She Answers

"Das! Das! Das! I wish you were here holding
my body and gently touching me—
Caressing the curves of the woman who belongs to
you, who will forever turn away everybody!
I close my eyes and remember when you spoke of
how much you truly loved me—
I wish all the people on this earth were gone leaving
just two—you and me!"

Looking at Janicah lying on the bed naked and listening to her scream his name, Das feels his sorrow grow. Invisible tears roll from his eyes. Even though he is without physical capabilities, he is cursed with memory. Tempted to rub Janicah's body, Das decides not to do so for no satisfaction would be given to her. Frustrated, Das sits in the corner and whispers to himself while watching Janicah.

He Speaks

"Hollow is the sound of a man desecrated by violent
storms of redemption—
Shallow be the depth of the still waters that flood the
hopes of relieving my tension!
Hollow is the heart that pushes life through the veins
and fuel to the muscles—
Shallow be the pond of virtue where I drowned that is
covered by thorny bushes!
A man is nothing more than a blink—he can be gone in
a matter of minutes or seconds—
His life is a merely a blur, unable to be captured scene-
by-scene like the cinemas.
In this dilemma, I am faced with the most venomous
creature known to man—denial—
In the meanwhile, I am bonded to the thoughts of loving
a woman who carries my child.
I am within feet of her reach, but I am millions of miles
away from being able to touch her skin—
While I was alive, death was my adversary, and now,
here we are together as the best of friends!
Am I blessed or condemned to knowing the woman
who loves me will love none other?
I await an answer while being smothered by the flames
of hell's kitchen, burning colder and colder!"

Realizing she's acting insane, Janicah throws on her clothes, staring unhappily in the mirror. Das stands behind her, desiring to provide her comfort. Once Janicah dries her eyes, she exits her room then storms down the steps, moping into the kitchen. Das stands in the entryway, watching as Janicah retrieves the eggs and milk from the refrigerator, the bread from the pantry, and a skillet from the cabinet, shaking his head. Stricken suddenly by memories of cooking breakfast for Das, Janicah closes her eyes, speaking as if she's aware of his presence.

She Answers

"I remember how you held my waist as we
together tasted all that I cooked—
How you kissed my neck, turned me around and
gave me your first, seductive look!
The crook we call life has robbed me of a stone
more valuable and precious of all gems—
Death must be a woman for she seduced and took from
me the greatest of all men!"

Das glides toward Janicah, acting out the memory of grabbing her waist and kissing her neck. Upset at the fact that he is without touch, he lowers his head and stands against the far kitchen wall, continuing to watch his sorrow-filled queen. Awakened from her trance, Janicah sighs deeply; however, Das's past plead of letting him cook for her helps her smile.

Finished with cooking breakfast, Janicah places her food onto the table. Upon sitting down, she blesses her food.

She Answers

"God, bless those like me who are without a reason
to give thanks for living—
The opportunity you've given me to breathe is a gift
that is no longer up lifting!
I ask that you bless the child I carry who waits the
moment to be born into this wilderness—
Let this food I eat aid in its strength and toughen each
part of his body that is filled with tenderness."

Following Janicah's prayer, Das sits in the chair across from her, shaking his head at the sorrowful beg. Slowly, he reaches out and cuffs his hands around Janicah's trembling hands. Although without an appetite due to the horrific events the day previous, Janicah forces herself to eat. As she nibbles at her eggs, Das stands to his feet then positions himself behind her.

He Speaks

> "Listen as I serenade you with a song that brings
> happiness to all who listen—
> Soon you will understand you are with everything
> you thought was lost and missing!
> Lift your brows and let your smile glisten through
> this tragedy-filled canyon—
> You are too meek to allow yourself to be defeated
> by this world or even the devil's antics!"

For nearly an hour, Das continues to watch Janicah weep at the kitchen table. Her whining increases with each thought of his death. Powerless, Das allows his guilt to send him into a whirlwind of fury. Uncontrollably, he punches the wall, affecting neither himself nor the innocent structure. After he gains control, he returns to his seat, counting the tears that glide from Janicah's eyes.

During that day and the months to come, Das continues to go through with Janicah her daily activities. Like an overprotective guard, he watches over her while she sleeps, while she bathes, while she goes to the market, and while she cooks. As time begins to heal Janicah's torn heart, her tears stemming from Das's absence lessens. Also, her frequent conversations with him wither. Nevertheless, there's not a day that pass where she doesn't kiss the jar of ashes.

11
Time to let go

Eight months has gone by, bringing Janicah to the beginning of her ninth month of pregnancy. The young lady who once weighed one-hundred and thirty-five pounds now weighs one-hundred and sixty. During a cold, January night, Janicah awakes from the pains of her child's kicking. Das knows she cannot hear him, but he asks how he can help anyway. Screaming in agony and pain, Janicah calls for her mother. "Mother!" she yells. Startled by her daughter's scream and, as quickly as her body allows her to move, Janicah's mother hustles to her daughter's aid.

"I'm here, Nicah!"

"It hurts!" Janicah yells, holding her stomach.

"Let's get you to your feet."

Carefully, Janicah's mother helps her daughter to her feet. Janicah nearly falls to the floor at the first attempt; however, her second attempt is a success. While hunching over and holding her stomach, Janicah feels a stream of fluid running down her legs. "Mother, it's time!" Janicah hollers. As if her life depends on it, Janicah's mother hurries her daughter to the stairs, ordering her to hold on to the handrail. Jaysen, Janicah's cousin who's been staying with the family for a month to help out around the house, waits for the ladies at the base of the stairs.

"You can do it, Janicah," Jaysen motivates.

"Nah—nah—not now," Janicah whispers to herself while clenching her stomach.

After successfully completing the fret of the first six steps, Janicah yells, "Das, where are you?" "I'm here," Das whispers from behind. "I'm right here, Janicah." Once Janicah and her mother reach Jaysen, Jaysen opens the door and escorts the two women through the blistering cold in to the carriage. Assured that his aunt and cousin are secured, Jaysen and Das mount the coach and orders the six horses to charge into the frigid darkness.

Immediately upon the arrival at the hospital, Jaysen carefully helps Janicah and her mother from the carriage. "Aunt Claire, go inside and grab someone," Jaysen orders. "I'll help Janicah."

"Alright. Just be careful with my baby."

Without hesitation, Janicah's mother hurries into the hospital, yelling for help.

"Someone please help us!"

At the sound of her cry, a young doctor, Dr. Menshe, approaches her.

"Madame, what's the matter?" he asks.

"It's my daughter. She's going to have a baby!"

"Where is she?"

"Outside," Claire points to the entrance.

Dr. Menshe calls his fellow staff members to the front of the hospital. Quickly, the assembled team follows Claire to the waddling, crying Janicah.

"We got it from here," Dr. Menshe assures Jaysen.

"Thank you," Jaysen gasps with fatigue.

Once a nurse helps Janicah into the wheelchair, the medical team rushes the screaming woman into the hospital, bringing her to the delivery room. Jaysen, Janicah's mother and Das hurry close behind.

Inside of the delivery room, two nurses help Janicah onto the bed then remove her undergarments. Janicah tosses in agony. Calm and collective, the doctor asks Janicah's mother to comfort her daughter by holding her hands and assuring her that everything will be alright. Hands shaking nervously, she does as directed. Aware of what's to come, Jaysen exits the noisy room and takes a seat in the waiting area. Das, on the other hand, watches helplessly from behind Dr. Menshe. Fed up with his queen's pain, he kneels next to Janicah's mother and tries to comfort his lady.

He Speaks

> "Don't worry, for I am here at your side to support you
> in the birth of our seed—
> Try to calm down for a moment and take deep breaths;
> breathe, my love, breathe!
> The time to let go of all aggression is now, so release
> it with your might and fury—
> I wish somehow you could see that I am here next to
> you; I wish you could somehow hear me."

With his hands between Janicah's legs, the doctor orders his patient to push. Streaks of sweat run down Janicah's face, joining the tears on the side as she does as she's ordered. Each series of exhausting pushes are followed by deafening screams.

"You're doing great," the doctor utters as he sees the head of the child. "I need you to continue pushing, Janicah. We're almost there!"

Janicah continues to push. Her mother continues to hold her hands. Das continues to watch. Near the brink of exhaustion, Janicah hollers, "Damn it, Das! Where are you?" "I'm here, Janicah," Das whispers while stroking his lady's head. "I'm right here."

After five hours of labor, Janicah gives birth to an eight-pound, six-ounce baby boy. Fatigued from the exhausting exercise of delivering a child, she eases to the bed, eyes swollen from crying. She looks at her mother and smile forcibly. Her mother mirrors her gesture. Also tired and hungry, the medical team becomes filled with joy as they watch as the doctor cut the umbilical chord and tap the child's bottom. At the sound of its cry, he wraps the new born in a white sheet then hand him to his mother. Following an array of congratulations, the doctor and his staff clean up their area then leave the happy mother and proud grandmother alone with the sleeping child.

"Congratulations," Janicah's mother smiles while rubbing her daughter's head.

"Thank you, Mother," Janicah smiles exhaustedly, sitting up with her son in her arms. "Isn't he so precious?"

"He is absolutely gorgeous. God has definitely blessed you!"

"He has blessed me," Janicah concurs as she looks down at her sleeping child. "He has blessed me in ways unimaginable."

In the midst of the mother and daughter conversation, Das hunches over Janicah, smiling proudly and staring wondrously at his son. Before he is able to say anything, Janicah whispers.

She Answers

"God took away the man I loved dearly, yet He blessed me with a child in your likeness—

His twinkling brown eyes, caramel complexion and
innocent smile reminds me of your gentleness and
kindness.
Damn you for leaving me while you journey through
the Lord's pastures of infinite bliss—
We will forever be united through our child who
will allow us the ability to communicate through our
spirits!"

Following Janicah's whisper, her mother recommences conversation.

"So Nicah, what name should become of this child?"

"Mother, I've decided to name him Das—Das Mi'Voir."

"Very well. Das Mi'Voir he shall be."

Janicah's mother kisses young Das on the forehead. "Young Das," she whispers, "you are the most precious of gifts that can be given to anyone." The cute child adjusts in his mother's arms.

"Nicah," Janicah's mother calls as she struggles to her feet.

"Yes, Mother."

"I'm going to leave you and your son alone. If you need me, I'll be outside in the waiting area with Jaysen."

"Okay, but get some rest."

"See you in a moment, my beautiful daughter."

Janicah's mother exits the delivery room, leaving the new mother and son the opportunity to get acquainted. Suddenly, baby Das cries. Weak and feeble, Janicah tries to calm her child down, yet nothing she does seems to work. At her wits-end, she gets ready to call for her mother. Bizarrely the child grows silent, eyeing the image before him. Sadden by the reality he is incapable of holding his child, Das kneels and smiles proudly at his creation.

"It will be you who will remove the hurt and agony that
pumps through your mother's heart—
I will watch over you as you become a man, and
your star when the day becomes dark.
So smart and gentle to a woman you will be, as you will
learn soon enough from your mother—

> You will be the reason why she smiles and why she can
> forget all the pains from that she has suffered.
> Love her as much as she loves you is the only request
> that I beg and ask of you—
> Oh how I pray for the opportunity to be given the
> strength and the ability to hold the two of you!
> Live merry, my son, for you will have no reason to
> fear the intents or deeds of man—
> Listen to the howls made by the night and watch the
> night's flickers for that is where I'll be found standing!"

Das kisses his child's head, and then, Janicah's cheek. After seeing the birth of his son, he is ready to part in peace. As he walks away, head lowered as if ashamed, Janicah calls his name.

"Das."

Das stares at Janicah. She stares back. Not sure if she can see him, Das replies.

"Janicah."

Unbelievably, Janicah responds with a head nod. Shocked and speechless, Das looks to the ceiling. A white light appears followed by a gentle, yet, deep voice.

> "You have been more devoted to this young lady
> than anything else in your life—
> For this moment only, I grant you the opportunity to
> hold your child and to tell Janicah goodbye.
> The window that allows this wish to be granted
> will close forever very soon—
> Therefore, I give you the ability to be heard only by
> Janicah and the opportunity to touch her and your son
> too!"

Astounded about what he just heard, Das slowly sits on the bed and cuddles with his family. Joy fills him although tears of happiness run down both his and Janicah's faces. Even though Janicah is unsure of Das is really next to her, she rests her head on his chest and listens to him whimper.

He Speaks

> "I was the wind that touched your face and the
> blanket that covered you while you slept—
> I was your warmth in the night and your strength
> you needed during my untimely death!
> The step it took for you to proceed was made possible
> by a firm, yet, gentle push—
> When complications wanted to keep you from living,
> it was I who gave you that needed tug.
> The love of a living heart never dies in death, it only
> grows stronger and stronger—
> I waited a long time to touch you again, and I would've
> have waited a lifetime longer.
> Amnesty has been granted to me by the Lord who
> controls all physical and all in spirit—
> I spoke to you in great lengths, hoping and praying
> that when I spoke you would hear it."

Das kisses the top of Janicah's head. Janicah snuggles in the cubbyhole made by his left side and responds.

She Answers

> "I wanted to believe that you were with me
> each sad day and every gloomy night—
> I thought it was you when I saw the flickering
> of each scented candle's light!
> I thought I lost the fight to unhappiness; now I
> realize I am triumphant—
> Don't leave me again, for I don't know whether
> I can make it over this hump again!"

He Speaks

> "Fear not the absence of my touch for I promise I will
> hold you forever and ever—

Since this is true, I want you to live life and receive all
the gifts that motherhood has to offer.
Welcome the breeze that surrounds your body for
it will be me holding and hugging you—
Do not curse the rains that fall from the clouds, for they
are my tears from madly loving you!
Listen to the music of the nights with the acoustics of
whispers, howls, whistles and roars—
It will be my speaking to you when you are doing
things that will cause your body to become sore.
Tonight and always, I will be the shore you visit, and
the horizon you gaze upon—
It is time for the dusk to leave so the day can welcome
the beautiful birth of a new dawn!"

Das bends forward and kisses Janicah's soft lips. Although her
eyes are closed, Janicah fights to stay awake. With all her might, she
forces her eyes open and stares into Das's subtle, brown eyes.

She Answers

"It feels like I am dreaming, but I know it is
you who is currently holding me—
How long will I be able to flourish in your presence
before it is time for you to go from me?

He Speaks

"Unfortunately, the ability you have to hear, see and
touch me will soon expire—
Yet, I will be watching you from the windows of
heaven's temple until we unite by God's fire!
I want you to sleep, my beautiful Janicah, for your body
has become weary and tired—
Just because you may not be able to hold me, that
doesn't mean our love for each other will ever retire!"

She Answers

"Sleep can wait for I am with sight to see the

beautiful face of my Heaven's angel—
The one who has freed me from hell's fingers that
had my mind and spirit mangled!"

He Speaks

"With each look at our child's face, I want you to
remember that he is a resemblance of me—
He will be the key that allows you to feel free, and the
hand that will always connect you to me.
He will be the answer to the question whether or not
you will ever love again—
He will aide you in your quest to find all that you want
inside of a loving husband.
Destiny has taught me that the road of everlasting
divinity has muddy detours and polluted streams—
If you are willing to challenge every obstacle, then you
will have the ability to receive all that you dream.
I walked on sun kissed terrains and swam infested
waters to find my love whose name is Janicah
Mi'Voir—
She is a constellation of stars, a goddess of intellect,
and the purity of heaven's brightest star!"

She Answers

"Once again your words command the attention of
my ears to listen—
Drowsiness could be the reason why I still feel
you are merely an apparition.
I look at our child who sleeps with no worries
and hasn't the slightest comprehension of hate—
He is surrounded by the love of his family, but it will be
me who is here when he finally awakes.
Before you are forced to abandon me, I want you to
know how I love you, love you so—
I am forever grateful to our Savior for allowing me this
closure before you must finally let me go."

Ellard Thomas

He Speaks

> "There is no gauge or ruler that can measure the
> amount of care or love I have for you—
> From now until I am prowling amongst the Lord's
> fields, I will always be there for you.
> When you speak, I shall listen and reply through the
> actions of our son—
> When I finally depart from your touch, don't cry
> yet smile, for my journey is finally done.
> Don't be like those living in shame who lower their
> chins at the slightest sign of defeat—
> Always stride with finesse, for you will forever be
> ordained as Janicah, Das Treymone's queen.
> I will be the wand that change your horrible nightmares
> to desirable and pleasurable dreams—
> I want to thank you for giving your heart to someone
> you've known for a moment, who now knows peace."

She Answers

> "I am going to close my eyes now, but I want you
> to continue speaking to me—
> Sing me a song that can strengthen my fragile heart
> and deplete its weakness and uncertainty.
> Kiss me once more so I will not forget the softness
> of your soft, moist lips—
> I am happy to know that I was with a man who's strong
> heart and mind can hoist ships."

Das curls down and kisses Janicah's dry lips. Realizing she is sound asleep, he gently lays her against a pile of pillows then places young Das on her chest, covering them both with a blanket. Following a deep sigh, he steps back and whispers.

He Speaks

> Each path on which I've walked and ever brutal
> obstacle I've encountered was worth its weight in
> pain—

If it would allow me to be with a woman like you, I
would without question relive it all again.
Sleep well, my sweet, for the future holds tricks and
treats along with frights and uncertainties—
I am happy that God has blessed these hands with a
moment's ability to hold my family.
The time has come where I must say goodbye and for
you to let go of your sorrows—
Let the events of yesterday guide you as you enter
into the wonders of tomorrow.
When we meet again, it will be at the altar of the Lord's
holy temple, looking into each other's soulful
windows—
When complexity overwhelms you, I will try my
hardest to make everything simple.
Sleep, my gentle queen, for your reasons to weep and
hurt will soon be over—
I will be the touch that brings you warmth when
the winter days grow from cold to colder."

Das kisses Janicah and his child once more. Shortly after, the bright light reappears followed by the voice. "It is time, now come, my son." Das backs a few steps away from the bed, smiling at his family. Upon closing his eyes and throwing open his arms, he and the light disappears.

After being asleep for an hour, Janicah awakes to a warm breeze and a familiar cologne essence. "Das," she calls, surveying the room for his whereabouts. "Das," she whines. Sadly, she receives no reply. Firm hold on her child, and very carefully, Janicah sits up and begins to cry. Yet, looking down at her child's smile, the flow of tears shut off as she smiles at her God-given gift.

Following a soft knock on the door, Janicah's mother enters the room. She sits in the chair next to the bed.

"How are you, Nicah?" she asks.

"I'm well," Janicah answers, eyes focused on the ceiling.

Filled with curiosity, Janicah's mother looks up at the ceiling and tries to find that which has her daughter's attention.

"What are you looking at, Janicah?"

"A mystery, Mother."

Seeing nothing but a bumpy ceiling, Janicah's mother shakes her head then kisses the crown of her daughter's head.

"Nicah," Claire whispers as she looks at her grandson, "Das will forever be with you. I'm sure wherever he is, he's watching you and his son. Therefore, be happy and cheerful for a death as brought a new life!"

With an ear-to-ear grin, Janicah kisses her mother on her cheek. "I know," she replies. "I know."

While smiling and looking down at her child, Janicah hears a faint voice.

He Speaks

"Hold no grudges with time for it is the best doctor
to heal every broken heart—
Remove the bars that hold captive vengeful intents
for they will soon tear you apart.
Remember when it is dark, I will be the dim light
guiding you to a place of safety—
Enjoy the blessings of each day until the day comes
when you will again be obligated to face me.
You have no reasons to be empty for the belly of your
hurt, by this time, should now be gone—
No longer shall you quarrel with your emotions nor
shall you beg for the absence of the sun.
The smile of a new day shines upon the head of
a woman so wonderful and so great—
Bathe in the happiness of the summers and ignore the
winter's hunger as you continue to achieve.
With every breath God allows you to take, be grateful
unlike those whom are wicked and cursed—
No longer shall you cry! No longer shall you grieve!
No longer shall you again hurt!"

Janicah nods. Afterward, she looks at her mother.

"Mother, I no longer hurt due to Das's death for I know he is well. Oddly enough, I had a dream that he was right here holding his son and me. That was definitely a weird dream."

"Perhaps, Janicah," Janicah's mother utters as she rubs her daughter's head, "this was no dream. Maybe, somehow or someway, God had allowed him to be with you once more!"

Janicah ponders her mother's comment for a moment, smiling at the possibly that she is right. Following a quaint look at the ceiling, she smiles at her son, closes her eyes and whispers to Das.

She Answers

> "If you can hear me, please listen to the rhythm
> made by my loving heart—
> Beating with encrypted codes of I love you that only
> you have the ability to decipher.
> Thank you for freeing me from the anguish that held
> me deep within its captivity—
> To me you will always be the star I wish upon, and our
> memories will be my gravity.
> Tell God I appreciate the gift of our son who I will
> love and cherish from now until death—
> It was you who gave me the strength necessary to
> extend my leg and accomplish my first step.
> I will never forget you, nor will our son grow without
> knowing about his father—
> Some will speak of you as an average man, but I will
> interject and speak of you as a martyr.
> May you be in peace as you lay in the comfort
> and care of our heavenly Father's bosom—
> You've shown me how much I was winning when I
> thought I was running only to lose.
> Goodbye, my prince, for the time to smile has
> come; therefore, I will be happy—
> Later we will be as one, but for now I must say I love
> and goodbye, and continue on the path I seek!"

Janicah lies down with her child on her chest. Her mother pulls a blanket over them then returns to the chair, falling asleep merely moments after. Quietly, Jaysen enters the room. At the sight of the sleeping family members, he returns to the waiting area.

Since that unexplainable night, time continues its mission. As the days turn into months, Janicah enjoys the challenges of motherhood, waking up in the middle of the night and attending to her child's needs. Yet, each morning, she sits young Das on her lap and tells him stories about his father. Following two years of storytelling and on the anniversary morning of Das's death, Janicah points to the jar of ashes.

"Who's that Das?" she asks.

Baby Das claps his hands and says, "Dat's daddee."

"What's daddy's name?"

Young Das stares at the jar for a moment then answers, "Me and daddee is Das!"

Final Thought

The story of *He Speaks She Answers* serves as a reminder that everyone lives a life of uncertainty; yet we are not doomed for living. Although Das experienced many challenges in his life, his will to be a better man for a woman was stronger than any force he could ever imagine. Although he suffered a brutal death, he didn't die empty. From the moment he received word from Janicah, he was immediately filled with love and hope—two attributes he didn't have prior to her letter. Fortunately, it was uncertainty that allowed him to capture all that he desired, setting him on a path of joy. As his death may have seemed untimely, he lived happier in a few months than he had in a lifetime. Thus, the morale of this story: Do not let uncertainty hinder you from capturing your dreams and desires; allow it to motivate you to achieving all you wish. Seek all that you desire and you shall find all that you seek! Allow the past to be a motivator for change, not a hindrance of exploring the future.

About The Author

"I am the soul of misfortune; a victim of night horrors.

Although I no longer cry, my heart still weeps.

Insomnia is the last of my worries; death is eminent—the anger I possess is not heart, but plasma deep.

Though this body is filled with memories of abuse, my mind is clear—a translucent vase saturated in malignity.

Look through my eyes and into my mind and see a child who dreams to be a man of serenity.

Ellard Thomas

Author of *He Speaks She Answers*, written with the influence of Shakespeare's tales, Ellard Thomas grew to be a rose from being embedded in the soil of a disastrous past. Since he was a young child, poetry has always been a part of his life. As his trials and tribulations grew, so did his poetic creativity. Incredibly, Ellard's loath for his odious past spawned his love to write, leading to his first published piece *He Speaks She Answers*, and his highly anticipated *Smiles from a Crying Child*. When asked *what is your greatest fear and accomplishment*, Ellard had this to say: "I fear that I may one day fail to see my greatest achievement; however, my greatest accomplishment is knowing that I have touched the lives of many who'll all become greater than I!"

Currently residing in Seattle, Washington, Ellard continues his efforts to support young writers and poets in their quest to be published authors.